S0-CEZ-615

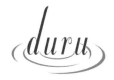

DOLMABAHÇE PALACE

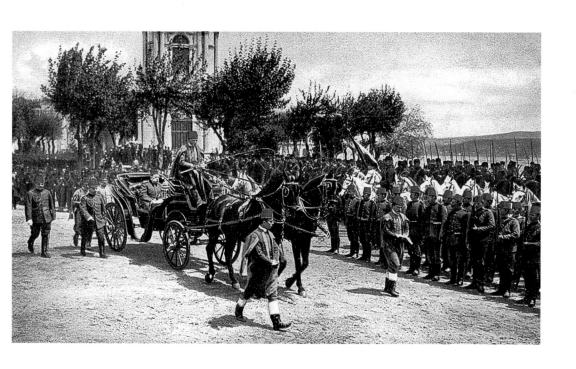

Pega 15

Pega 39

Pega 37

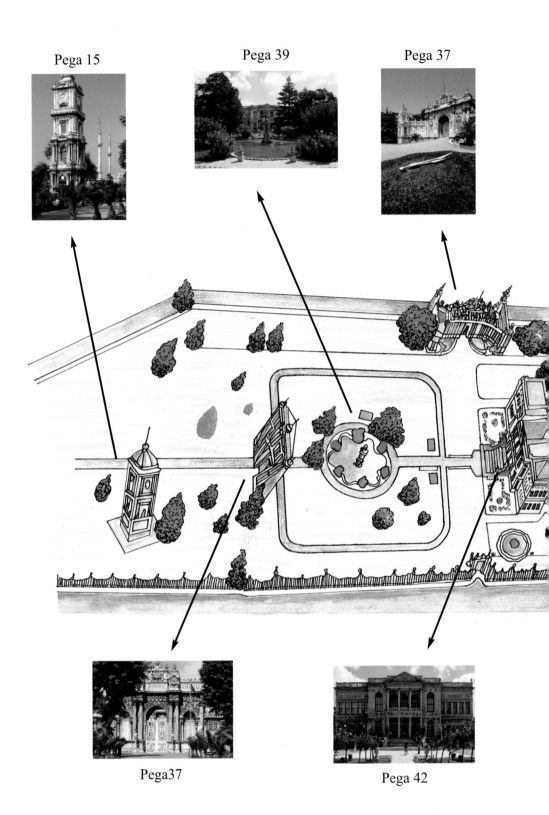

Pega37

Pega 42

Pega 39

Pega 73

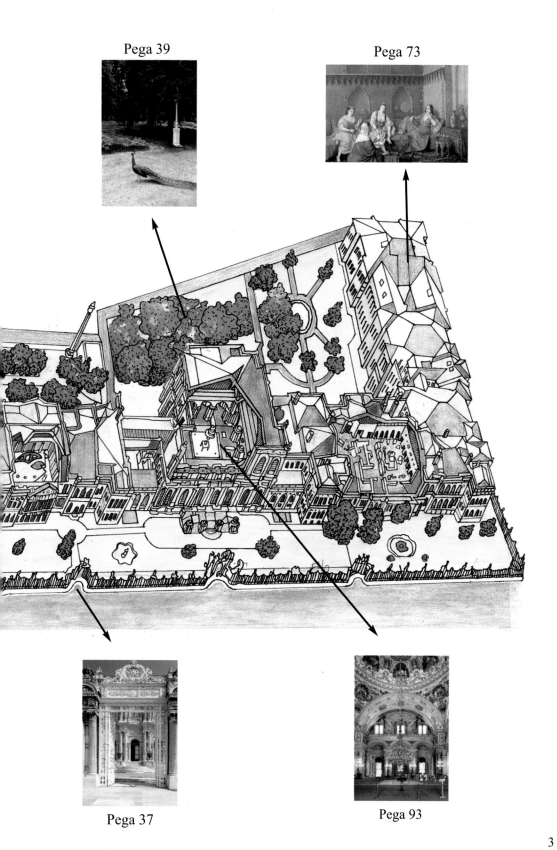

Pega 37

Pega 93

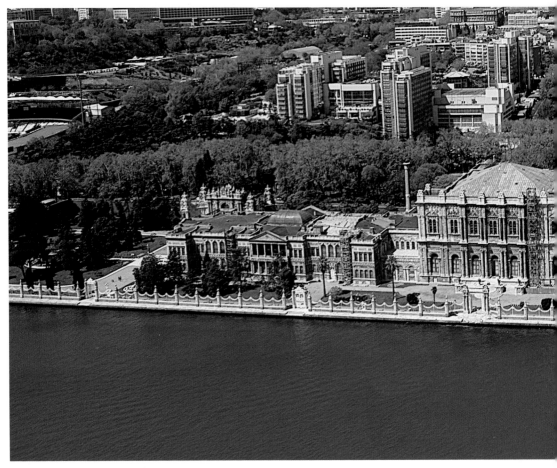

Dolmabahçe Palace

Section 1

PALACE CONCEPT AND TRADITION IN THE HISTORY OF THE TURKS

As is known, the first division among the human societies was governed by the environment they lived in. People who lived in regions with a relatively regular rainy climate were organized as "agricultural societies" while those living in regions without such conditions were gathered in "shepherd societies". While the agricultural societies developed their watering channels and achieved substantial progress in production techniques, "shepherd" or "nomadic" societies stayed within a static organizational system to a great extent. It was only during the relatively "new" period of the history that these two types of society were merged and societies were occupied with both agricultural activities and stockbreeding. However, the adventures of the human society thereafter were marked by its social features which had become inherent to humankind until then.

The Turks have their origins exclusively in the tradition of "shepherd" or "nomadic" so-

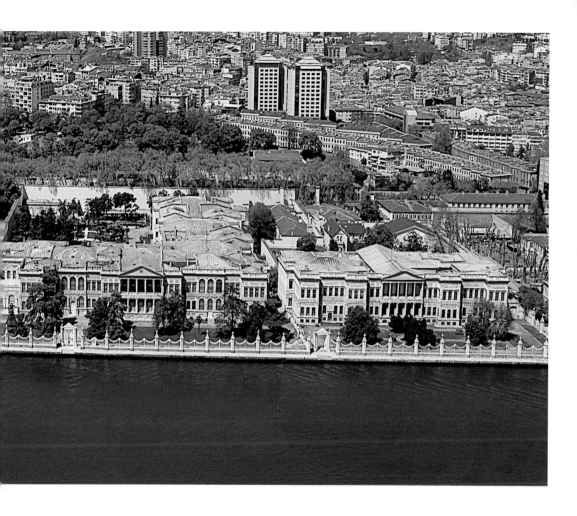

ciety. They tended flocks of goat and sheep on the broad plains of Middle Asia and during the times of great drought – hence famine – they fought for life by launching raids on the surrounding countries, especially on the fertile plains of China. As a matter of fact, it is known that the Great Wall of China was built as a means of protection against the raids of the Turks. This period of nomadic life dating back to thousands of years of known history brought about certain customs and traditions that still affect the life of the Turks. The experience, the abilities and a series of features that they gained through the incredibly arduous journeys they made to find grassland and sources to water and to feed their herds continued to deeply influence their lifestyle even after they shifted to settled life.

The nomadic life is monotone and simple besides being very difficult. The nomad who is nearly always tired because of long journeys and continuous struggle does not let any sophisticated details into his life. In order to survive in his difficult life, he carries two basic features that are fed by the same root: practicality and pragmatism. For this reason, the concept of "palace" did not take place in the history of Turks until the modern times in the sense that is known in the West. Hun Atilla who ruled over an endless empire that extended from

Pacific Ocean to the inner parts of Europe, as well as Cengiz Khan who founded the greatest and the most powerful state of his age lived in "otag" which consisted of the combination of several tents instead of palaces like many other rulers. It is known that Cengiz Khan spent most of his life inside a mobile "car-house" that is pulled by buffalos and oxen. Such a residence of course can not be defined as a "palace".

The kings and emperors who ruled on "agricultural societies" in the regions neighboring Turks dwelled in the most glorious palaces of their age. Both the Chinese Empire and Byzantine Empire lived in giant palaces that consisted of hundreds or thousands of rooms and halls. Persian and Arabic civilizations of the Middle East also built giant and magnificent palaces. The beauties

Osman Gazi

and grandeur of Baghdad palaces are told by the historians of the period in Arabian Nights. The Alhambra Palace in Spain is considered one of the biggest and the most beautiful palaces of a certain period. With central kingdoms emerging in the west, the concept of multi-roomed palace developed rapidly. Buckingham, Versailles, Tuileries and many other palaces are among the examples of this.

For centuries, Turks did not feel such a necessity as the "practical and pragmatic" features of the nomadic society prevented them from doing so. They lived in complexes that consisted of rooms with different functions.

Like his father Ertuğrul Gazi, Osman Gazi, the founder of Ottoman Empire was the leader of nomadic Kayı horde and is known to have spent most of his life in the tent. Orhan Gazi, who moved the center of the state from Söğüt to Bursa, lived in a large mansion and did not settle in the palace of the Byzantine tekfur or elsewhere. The palace built in Edirne, the second largest capital of Ottoman Empire was merely a large mansion though it was called a palace. Mehmet II (Fatih), the conqueror of Constantinopolis, one of the largest cities of 15th century, while making it the capital by changing its name to İstanbul, preferred staying at his otag for a long period, instead of settling down in the splendid palaces of the Byzantine Empire. Afterwards, he lived in a large mansion which was named as the Old Palace that was erected at the district known as Beyazıt today.

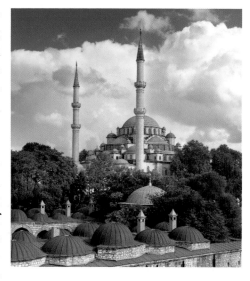

Fatih Mosque

The first large palace complex of Ottoman Empire was the Topkapı Palace. The palace, which Fatih Sultan Mehmet ordered to be built during his last years on a point overlooking the view of the historical peninsula, does not correspond to the classical concept of palace. It does not have an architectural unity and it consists only of some chalets within the same garden besides some auxiliary buildings. Contrary to the claims of some malicious historians and interpreters, such a type of construction was not due to the Ottomans' lack of knowledge, ability and vision, but because they did not have a tradition of palace in the western sense. As a matter of fact, during the same period of Fatih Sultan Mehmet, the Fatih Mosque which is among the most beautiful and magnificent buildings of today's İstanbul was built, to prove the invalidity of the abovementioned opinion.

Topkapı Palace was further constructed with various mansions built by the sultans who ruled after Mehmet II. However, as stated above, because these extensions do not go with each other due to their different architectural styles, they clearly do not form a "whole" in the sense of architectural history.

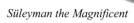

Süleyman the Magnificent

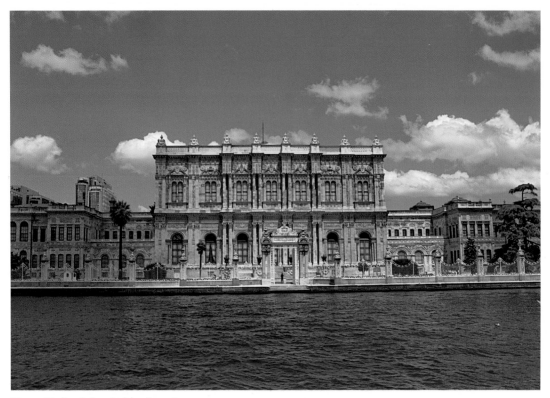

View of Dolmabahçe Palace from the

Sinan, one of the greatest three architects of our world and of the history of civilization, was carrying out his giant and extraordinarily beautiful works, the symbols of the grandeur of Ottoman Empire at this period. However, Sultan Süleyman the Magnificent known as "the great Turk" in Europe, had Koca Sinan build only some side buildings, kitchens and stables to his formal residence, Topkapı Palace. In those structures, functionality became more important than appearance and grandeur.

Such attitude may be seen as a reflection of the lifestyle of the Turks' nomadic past that still prevails after centuries, which might well explain their lack of attention to grandeur and appearance. However, things began to change in the 19th century; the Ottoman diplomats and statesmen who visited Western countries started to convey and share the information and experience they gained and then the presence of different locations and lifestyles was comprehended. Abdülmecit I was raised under the training of his French governess brought to palace by his French grandmother Nakşidil Sultan (maiden name Aimée Dubuc de Rivery). Since the first years of his rule, he started to think about building a large palace of Western style and attracted close attention and encouragement from his mother Bezm-i Alem Valide Sultan. To fulfill his dream, he had only 3 years to wait until 1842.

Section 2

BEFORE THE CONSTRUCTION OF THE PALACE...

Bezm-i Alem Valide Sultan, mother of Sultan Abdülmecid was highly interested in construction and building. Among the works that she ordered to be built, there is the Guraba Hospital, a health institution for the needy that still operates successfully, and Bezm-i Alem Valide Sultan School (named today as İstanbul Girls' School). Besides Dolmabahçe Mosque which is also at Dolmabahçe, Dilkusa Summer House at Yıldız Palace, three different Bezmialem Valide Sultan Fountains at Maçka, Topkapı and Yıldız as well as the first Galata Bridge built of wood on Haliç are also among her charity works.

The area of the palace today was a gulf and port settlement used mostly by the Ottoman navy between the 15th and 17th centuries. However, starting from this date, the region sinking rapidly into marshes and the alluviums brought by the river made it unusable. When the condition began to influence the nearby neighborhoods (Beşiktaş, Fındıklı, etc.) negatively, the old port that turned into marshes was immediately filled. Thus beautiful mansions and waterside houses were built in the wide area that was gained. With some construction works during the period of Ahmet III (1703-1730), some existing buildings were extended, repaired, connected together and a beautiful summer palace was thus built with the name Beşiktaş Saray-ı Humayunu at the location of the palace today. While Sultan Selim III and Mahmud II actually resided at Topkapı Palace, they rather used Hasbahçe at this area and this waterside palace during summer. However, when Abdülmecit ascended the throne, the mansions of

Dolmabahçe Palace and Mosque

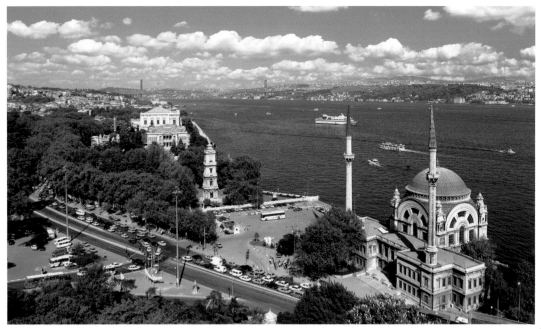

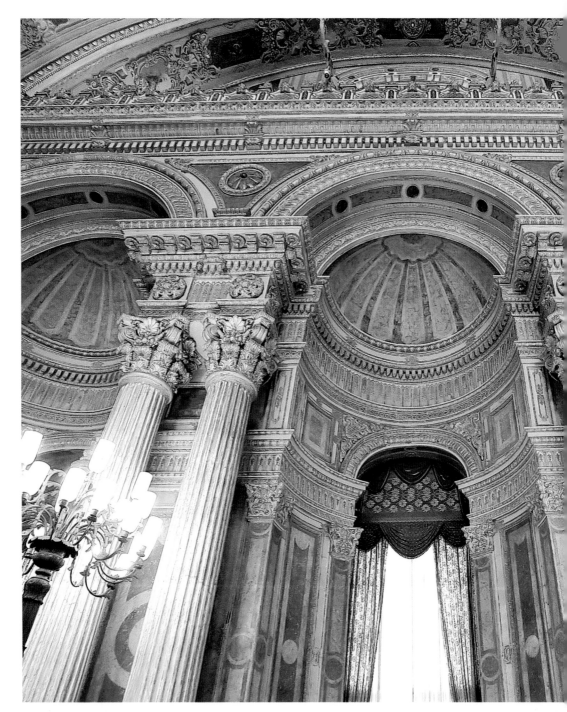

the wooden summer palace were worn out and out of use. Upon this, a large area was gained by tearing down this great mansion and waterside houses and this location was set as the location of

Dolmabahçe palace.After a short inquiry, it is revealed that Abdülmecit decided to assign Karabet Amira

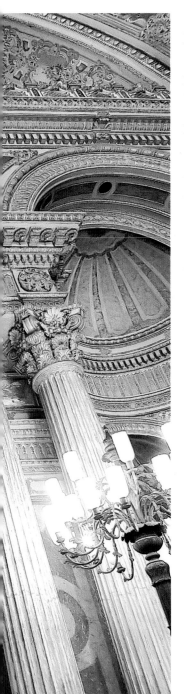

Balyan as the architect for the construction works of the palace. However, in the official documents of the palace, Abdülhalim Efendi is recorded as the head architect and İsmail Zühtü Paşa is the architect and trustee of the building. Karabet Balyan is stated as authorized in construction. It should be assumed that Karabet Balyan, who was the main responsible person of the work carrying its load, also received the advice of Abdülhalim Paşa. Also it is understood from various sources that the opinions were consulted of many architects who had great experiences in mansion and waterside houses which was highly improved during that period.

Karabet Balyan was at the end of his forties and the elder son of an Armenian family who had five generations of experience in construction and architecture. He had a good training and when he was young, he traveled around nearly all of Europe, especially France and England, and made observations. He spent the last ten years of his life on constructing mansions and waterside houses to Ottoman statesmen, that is to pashas, and acquired an important experience. There was a general opinion that he was the most famous architect of his period. When Karabet Balyan accepted this duty, his son Nigogos had reached the point of a master after a long period of foremanship. He was the most important helper of his father during all the phases of the construction work that lasted twelve years.

It is generally accepted that the construction of the palace was started in the spring of 1843. At this date, the demolition of the buildings that were still standing of the old palace, which was started in 1842, was not completed yet. The two works continued together for a while and demolition and rubble removal continued on the one side, while the works for laying the foundation went on on the other side. Also, as the plan was determined and improved, some confiscations were carried out in order to add new lands needed for the property and the cemetery nearby was transferred elsewhere thus widening the working area.

Some witnesses of the period point out that the young sultan frequently came to supervise the works and intervened in the architectural plan. However, it would be correct to think that these were merely details and that they did not really have an effect.

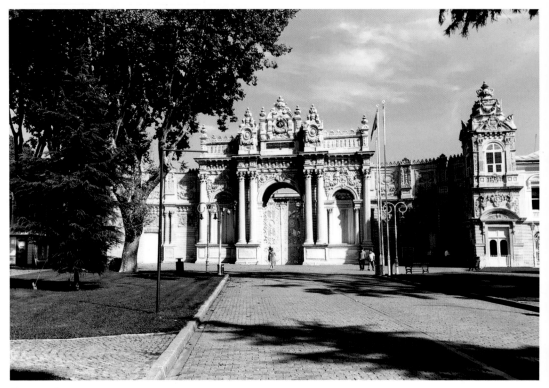

Treasury Door

Section 3
THE CONSTRUCTION OF THE PALACE AND ITS STYLE...

The palace consists of three parts (Mabeyn-i Humayun, Muayede lounge and seraglio) as well as the secondary buildings, that is auxiliary buildings where the needs of the residents of the palace were met. At first the port, 600 meters in length was constructed and the first three buildings that constitute the main section were formed. The tall walls surrounding the palace were constructed after the main buildings were completed.

It is accepted that the rough construction of the main building was completed in 1847. This is reflected on the small boards ornamented with the signature of the sultan. While the work continued with the construction details and ornamentation of the sections afterwards, the construction of attached buildings also started at the same time. The three monumental gates over the high wall surrounding the building (Saltanat Gate, Valide Gate and Treasury Gate) were completed with the rest of the construction and the palace was open to service when the sultan and his family moved here in 1856.

Despite all its beauty and the attention given to the construction, Dolmabahçe Palace is much smaller than its large examples in Western countries. It is understood from the events and talks of some historians that the sultan shared the same opinion. However, because it

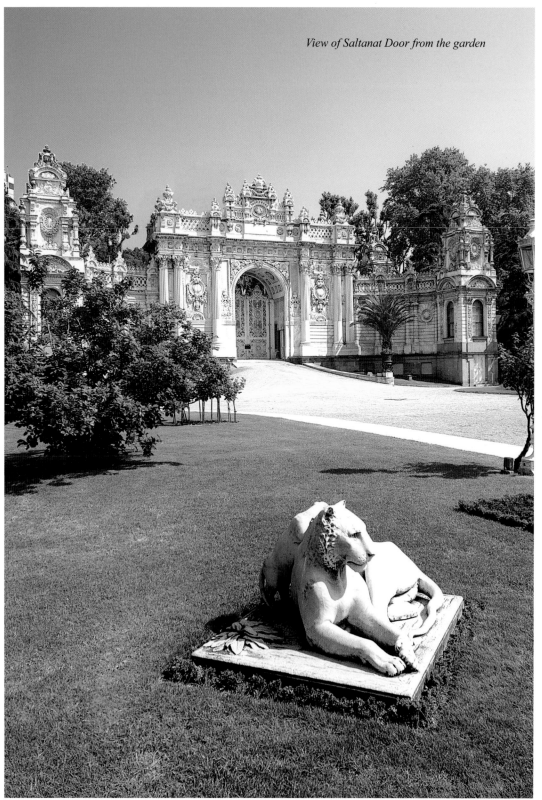

View of Saltanat Door from the garden

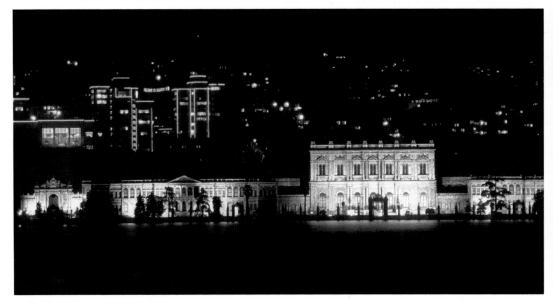

The night view of the palace from the sea

was a period of great financial trouble, it is known to have brought a great burden to the budget. The Crimean War with Russia that took place between 1853 and 1856 left the Ottoman finance in a condition to be compelled to borrow money for the first time. Spending a part of the outside support provided as such made the burden even heavier on the financial structure of the government which was already in trouble. However, political and diplomatic imposition which was the most important feature of the period could explain a little the necessity of the fortune spent in the construction of the palace, the amount of which is not really known, but helped the empire to stand relatively as strong as possible due to its importance in the world politics and protocol.

The period of Abdülmecit is noteworthy not only due to this palace, other mansions and summer houses that were made with large costs, but also with the prodigality that the palace life reached. The young sultan who did not receive a proper education during his life as a prince escaped from the financial and political troubles that got heavier, ignored them gradually and gave into alcohol. Abdülmecit who was caught in tuberculosis disease at an early age could only live at this beautiful palace for five years and then died at an early age in 1861.

It is not possible to attribute the architectural style of Dolmabahçe Palace to any style that is known. It is certain that the reason for this is both the synthesis concept of the architects and the exterior effects of the period. It is because in the building and the construction of the palace, the famous Turkish-Ottoman masters as well as the foreign experts and masters brought from abroad carried out different works. For such reasons, in the palace, there is a harmony of rococo, empire and baroque lines. Also the style that is shaped by many rooms opening to wide halls is a feature of traditional Turkish-Ottoman house which is open and known. Thus, the architecture of the palace is defined as an "eclectic" concept.

When one looks at the palace from the sea, the high section in the middle is Muayede, that is, the large ceremony hall. Seraglio building is on the Beşiktaş part, Mabeyn-i Humayun or Selamlık (the part of a large Muslim house reserved for the men) is located on the left. Just after the Treasury Gate on this side, there is Dolmabahçe Mosque that the mother of the sultan had ordered to be built in baroque style to the same architect, Karabet Balyan, including the thinnest minaret in the world as well as the clock tower. Abdülhamit II had assigned the construction of this clock tower to the palace architect of the period, Sarkis Balyan between 1890 and 1895 in neo-baroque and empire style. The structure that is extended in the background to gain a reverse L plan to the whole of the main building is the Concubine Chamber.

The architects, considering that the location of the palace was gained through filling the sea, took some precautions before starting the construction in order to avoid any partial collapse that would occur in time on the ground or sliding towards the sea due to the immense weight of this ground. Accordingly, thousands of oak poles were nailed to be placed on the rock ground under the fill material prior to construction. Over the surface like the "back of a hedge log", a ground cover was paved made of an intense plaster over 1 meter thick and strengthened with a wooden grill and the construction in its unique sense was carried out over this ground.

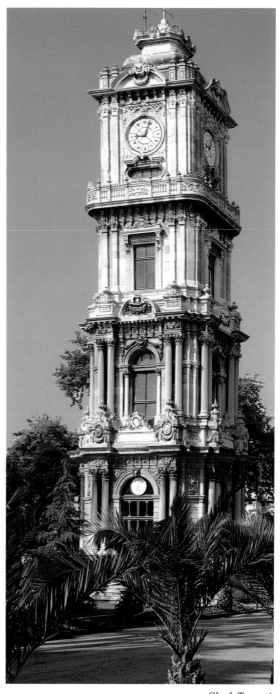

Clock Tower i

The building has a composite structure. Accordingly, the walls are made up of biscuit (twice-baked) bricks and formed by trimmed stones with carriage feature from the outside. Dividing the heavy weight on the columns enabled both these columns and the facade ornaments to be carried out with extraordinary grace and finesse. This stone material is mostly acquired from the stock quarry nearby Istanbul and it is also known that some stone material

15

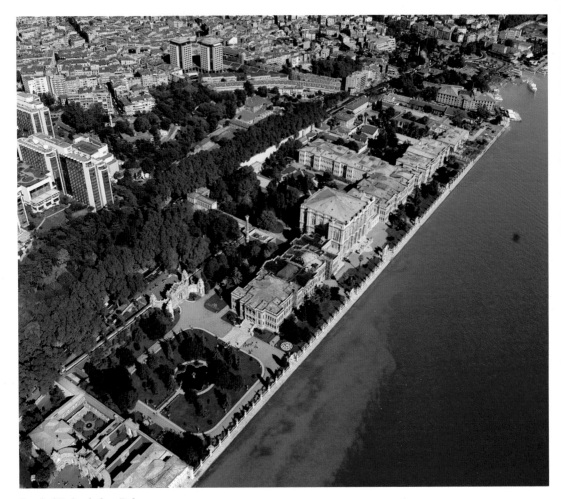

Roof of Dolmabahçe Palace

used was brought with ships from France and Italy. Most of the white marbles used in the facade cover of the building is taken out from Prokonessos stock quarry in Marmara Island, shaved and cut in its place and transferred by barges. Also, even though in small quantities, a certain amount of colored marble – especially pink and vague green/blue- was brought from Egypt and Italy to be used in the construction.

While the roof of the sections Mabeyn-i Humayun and Seraglio are of wooden origin and covered with lead, the ceiling of Muayede Lounge is covered with a wide and vaulted dome application with a traditional Turkish-Ottoman roof cover. Upon this, here again a roof is situated with a wooden material. The outer part of this roof is covered with lead like in large mosques and Mabeyn-i Humayun and Seraglio sections with a lead cover to prevent the humidity and permeability (the reason that lead is chosen as a covering material is because melted lead can easily be applied to roof repairs).

Section 4
ORNAMENTS OF THE PALACE AND OTHER FURNISHINGS...

In the ornamentation of Dolmabahçe Palace, as in the other palace and mansions of the period, it can be said that the European effect is dominant, but is in harmony with the most beautiful examples of Turkish-Ottoman ornamentation art. The art of ornamentation is an important element that shows the culture and art concept of a nation. In the basis of this, there are motifs. Motifs are the symbols of the art of a nation. Within the Turkish ornamentation art, the Rumi or Selçuki motifs have a dominant feature. In those motifs, many figures of animals, especially the birds, and flowers have priority. Besides, there are dragons and some other imaginary creatures. However, because of the prohibiting attitude of Islam towards these motifs, figures of flowers are rather dominant. All these effects are clearly seen in the ornamentation of Dolmabahçe palace. As a matter of fact, ornamentation elements with dominant decorative elements can be observed more.

In the outer ornamentation of the palace, rosettes, medallions, oyster shells, crowns and especially in composite characters (ion/Corinth), columns with channels are used. In all these ornamentations, besides the most important Turkish-Ottoman artists of the period, the most successful Western and Eastern artists of the period were employed.

In the inner ornamentation of the palace, a ceiling and wall embellishment named as engravings (kalemişi) is seen. These are irreplaceable elements of Turkish-Ottoman ornamentation. This is the name given to the colorful ornamentation over straight or curvy structure

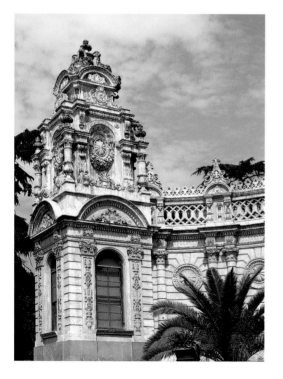

surfaces such as vault or dome, over a dried plaster with a thin brush. The applications of illumination that are at least as important as these are also striking. Illumination means "gilding", and it is not only done with color but also with paint. This traditional Turkish-Ottoman art seen in the ornamentation of hand-written Kur'an and other written works' page margins is used widely in the inner ornamentation of Dolmabahçe Palace. However, the western influence that affected all areas of art in the 19th century is also reflected in illumination. Flower motifs that are used as single in classical period are seen as bouquets inside vases in the ornamentation of the palace.

The golden gild that is frequently used in the inner ornamentation of the palace is a

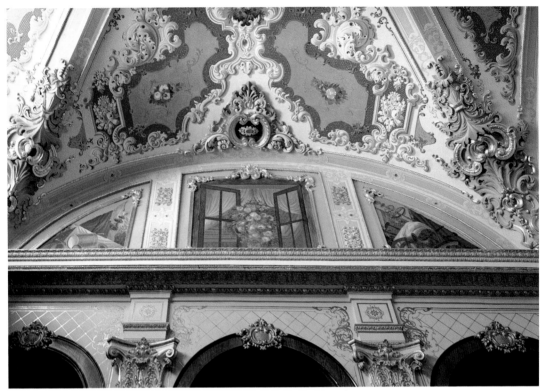

Ceiling ornamentation

Turkish-Ottoman ornamentation style with some of its techniques. The golden gild is the name given to the gold cut in thin lines and beaten down between the membrane taken out of cattle's intestines and turning the gold into transparent leaves. It is said that the amount of gold used in the inner ornamentation of Dolmabahçe Palace is three tons. It is not certain but even this can give an idea about the abundance of the golden gilds used in the ornamentation.

All these techniques of ornamentation have been carried out by the most famous Turkish-Ottoman, Iran and Afghan masters of the period. However, we need to mention the Sechan who worked on the ornamentation as well as the pavement and the covering of the ground. This French master who carried out a serious duty like the ornamentation of the bedrooms of sultan and her mother gained his fame with the works he carried out at Paris Opera. Sechan did not only carry out these works, but also produced some of the furniture at his workshops in France (Turgot).

The material used in the pavement of the floor is actually telescopic oak parquet. Paving these parquets produced in various tones of brown gave all the floors of the palace a beautiful and decorative effect. Besides these oak parquets, it is known that parquets of linden tree, walnut and other wooden materials were used. It is clearly seen that these ground pavements have an explicit harmony with the mahogany and walnut doors.

Most of the furniture in the palace was produced at various carpenters and workshops in İstanbul during the course of the construction. However, it shall be stated that also many were brought from West and East. It is possible to guess the number of the furniture used in such a palace that stretches over nearly 14600 m2 with 285 rooms and 43 lounges. Some of the furniture and goods used in the palace consisted of gifts brought from Iran, China, India, Afghanistan and Egypt. All these provided an eclectic result in the palace where Western architecture is dominant.

Almost all of the carpets, weaving and curtains of the palace are prepared in the carpet house and foundry in Hereke. Most of the carpets are products of Hereke and there are also carpets of Uşak, Manisa, Gördes and Kayseri among them. In the weavings, just like in the carpets, most of the products are from Hereke, but there are specific cloths from Eastern cities as well. European weaving was also used however rarely.

The vases, crystal goods and silverware may be mentioned among the most important elements of the ornamentation of the palace. In the illumination of the parlour and rooms, many chandeliers have been used made of Baccarat crystals which were quite popular at the time. Besides, though fewer, there are some crystal chandeliers that were made in Murano and produced in England. Again in the illumination, it is seen that high crystal chandeliers are used, especially at the beginning of the stairs. Usage of silverware is wide spread. Silver chandeliers, plates, braziers and tableware form collections that are unique in wealth.

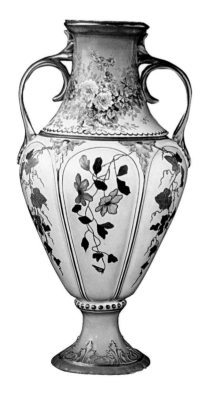

In the decoration of the palace, it is seen that many porcelain vases were used. Some of these beautiful works were brought from Eastern Asia countries (China and Japan) and some of them were produced from European manufacturers such as Meissen and Sevres. The rare and precious pieces brought from manufactures in Yıldız that started production towards the end of the century, have enriched this collection even more. Besides, beautiful clocks mostly brought from Europe and some of which were made in İstanbul have been used in enriching the inside decoration of the palace even more.

Before the palace was open to service, a magnificent ornamentation was carried out with the many beautiful paintings that were placed on the walls. These collections were even more enriched especially during the period of Abdülaziz. This duty was basically

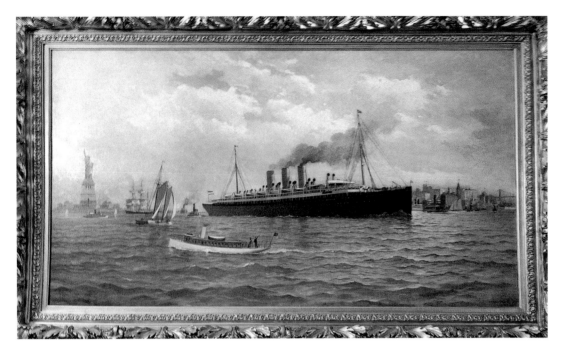

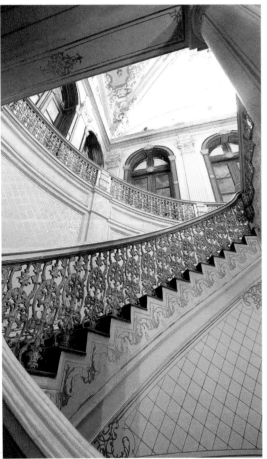

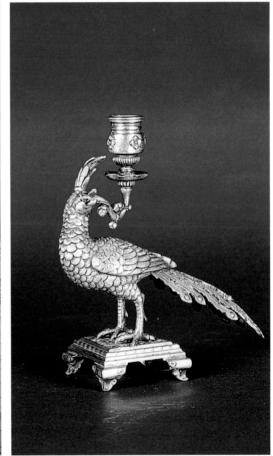

carried out by Şeker Ahmet Paşa, who was the artist of the palace and aide of the sultan, as well as his tutor Gérome de Goupil who had been in France. Thus, besides the imported works of famous artists such as Schreyer, Fromentin and Daubigny, the works of famous artists who worked as the royal artist have taken their place in the parlor, room and corridors of the palace. Among these famous artists who produced works as the royal painter, French Guillemet and Polish Chlebowski as well as Russian Ayvazovski of Armenian origin may be mentioned. This perfect collection was enriched even further with the works of Italian Acquarone and again the Italian palace painter Austo Zonaro. Of course, the works of Turkish artists shall be mentioned: Osman Hamdi Bey, the founder of Turkish museum curation, as well as caliph Abdülmecit who is also a successful painter, Şeker Ahmet Paşa and the works of other Turkish artists of military origin have taken their place as important works.

At the period when the palace was put into use, the locations were heated especially with ceramic tile stoves, fire places and braziers. These beautiful ceramic tile stoves, fire places and braziers were also important decoration materials. However, due to its height as well as largeness as area, a different application was found necessary in the Muayede Lounge; with the hot weather that is provided with a heating system founded in the basement, the cold of the lounge was broken and a heating of 20 degrees was achieved. Later, during the period of   Sultan Mehmed Reşat, central heating was founded in all the buildings in 1910 and the palace was thus heated within the last period of the Empire.

The illumination element of the period was the coal gas used by the French technology.

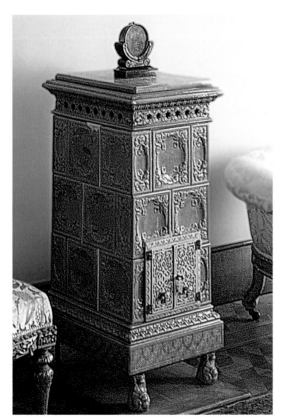

For this purpose, a "gashouse" was founded on a land just behind the football stadium of today (İnönü stadium) and the palace was illuminated with the coal gas provided from here. Upon seeing that excess gas could be produced at gashouse, street lighting started at Beşiktaş area. A second step of this gashouse application was the Small Gashouse that was made in Kuzguncuk and used in the illumination of Beylerbeyi palace.

However, because of the fear that the usage of coal gas could cause fire as well as some accidents in auxiliary buildings starting especially with the kitchen, the usage of electricity increased in time and some chandeliers that used to work with coal gas were turned into electrical systems.

Section 5

MASTERS OF THE PALACE...

Apart from Sultan Abdülmecit, Dolmabahçe Palace hosted 5 sultans (Abdülaziz, Murad V, Abdülhamit II, Mehmet Reşat V, Mehmet Vahidettin VI) and one Ottoman caliph. Even though Abdülhamit II stayed at this palace for a very short period, he should be mentioned among the "hosts", that is, the masters of Dolmabahçe Palace.

Sultan Abdülmecit and Sultan Abdülaziz were the sons of Mahmut II. All four of the sultans who ruled after Abdülaziz were the sons of Abdülmecit. Abdülmecit Efendi who had the caliph title for a short time after regality was removed and who was the last member of Ottoman Dynasty as a religious authority was the son of Sultan Abdülaziz. These sultans and caliphs shall be mentioned briefly.

SULTAN ABDÜLMECİT

Sultan Abdülmecit is the 31st sultan of Ottoman Dynasty. We have mentioned him briefly above while giving information about the making of the palace. Abdülmecit, who was born when his father Mahmut II was 38, took the throne while he was 16 upon the early death of his father. He can not be said to have received a proper education. During his childhood, Abdülmecit was tutored by French governess brought to the palace by Nakşidil Sultan (maiden name Aimée Dubuc de Rivery). He is known in history as the sultan who accelerated the Westernization movements that began during the period of Selim III. Especially Gülhane Hatt-ı Humayunu declared by Mustafa Reşit Paşa a few months following inauguration of Abdülmecit as well as the Administrative Reforms that he put into effect are accepted among the most important turning points of westernization attempts of the Ottoman Empire in near history.

The army of Mehmet Ali Paşa of Kavala, the governor of Egypt, defeated the Ottoman army severely at Nizip while Sultan Mahmut II was ill. Abdülmecit ascended the throne during such a difficult period. Upon the defeat at Nizip, the Russian navy arrived at Bosphorus using the door opened by Hünkar Port agreement and following this, the European countries (England, France, Russia, Prussia and Austria) were involved in the situation. The army of Kavalalı was stopped with London Conference (1840) and the Ottoman State received the support of great Western powers. With the agreement entered in 1841, the privileges of Russia provided with Hünkar Port agreement were put out of effect and its dominance over the straits was approved once again. This is accepted as one of the most important gains of Abdülmecit period.

Abdülmecit assigned the rule of the state to his viziers that he depended on especially with the advice of his mother Bezm-i Alem Valide Sultan and did not interfere with daily and routine management issues. He tried to forget and ignore the troubles especially about public finance by drinking heavily and in the arms of young and beautiful palace ladies. This

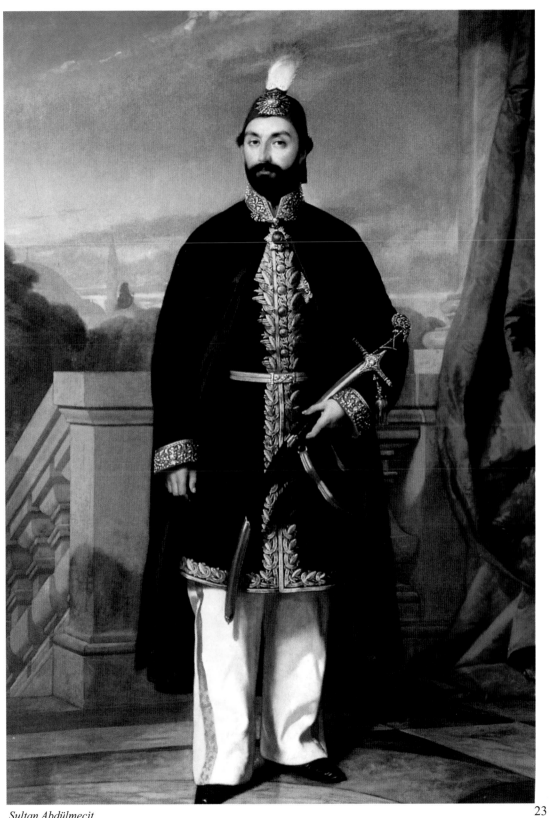

Sultan Abdülmecit

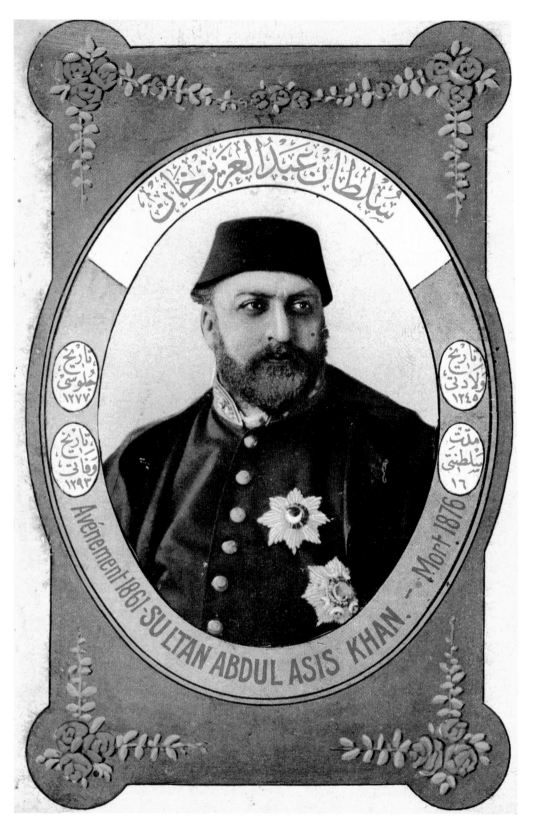

سلطان عبدالعزيز خان

تاريخ ولادتى ١٢٤٥

مدت سلطنتى ١٦

تاريخ جلوسى ١٢٧٧

تاريخ وفاتى ١٢٩٣

Avénement 1861 · SULTAN ABDUL ASIS KHAN. — Mort 1876

24

"fast" life resulted in being the father of many children (he had 23 daughters and 17 sons that we know of) and tuberculosis that he caught at a very early age. The medicine of the period was insufficient for his illness and besides his passion for drinking resulted with his death at a very early age, only when he was 38.

Sultan Abdülmecit was cultivated with an elegant attitude and no doubt with the influence of his governesses, thus he was open to Western norms. He had a theatre built next to the palace and gave substantial support to the cultural activities of the period. Ottoman Empire entering Crimean War (1853-1856) by making an alliance with big Western countries, England and France, also happened during his period. However, the Ottoman Treasury was not in a condition to overcome the heavy burden of such a war. The people of the palace, the sisters and nephews continuing a great consumption caused the young sultan to be helpless in many conditions. The first borrowing of money from the West happened during this period for this war.

The great reception and feast thrown by Abdülmecit upon the victory at Crimean War was carried out at Muayede lounge of the new palace, that is Dolmabahçe palace and it was opened to service with this occasion. However, as we have stated above, he could only live for five years at this palace that he had built with great attention and spending a lot of money. He died in İstanbul in June 1861 and was buried in his grave that he had reserved nearby the grave of Yavuz Sultan Selim.

SULTAN ABDÜLAZİZ

Sultan Abdülaziz who ascended the throne upon the death of Abdülmecit is the son of Mahmut II from Pertevniyal Hanımsultan like the late sultan who was his brother. He was only 31 years old at the time. Abdülmecit who did not receive a proper training and who suffered from this made sure that his brother Abdülaziz was trained as good as possible. He spoke French fluently and was interested in poetry and music. It is known that he was a composer as well as a good painter and he trained himself as a ship engineer. It is known that he himself drew the plans of some ships that he ordered for Ottoman navy. Abdülaziz was highly interested in all kinds of sports, but especially wrestling, horse riding and archery. He personally participated in the wrestling that he organized and wrestled with the most famous wrestlers of the period; he sometimes won and sometimes did not.

Some historians show Abdülaziz as a person who did not understand from state affairs, who did not care about it and who spent all his time with wrestling and other joyful activities. This is not really true. Abdülaziz was closely interested in public administration; however he could not take important steps that would be useful for the future of the state. His descending of the throne with a palace intervention led by Mithat Paşa is also due to the fact that he could not take these steps. He was actually a person very much interested especially in navy issues. He put great effort to adapting the Ottoman Navy to the conditions of his time. He modernized nearly all the weapons of the army and supplied it with the cannons and guns of the latest model. However, because the possibilities of the public finance were restricted, he preferred to get into debt with European banks and Galata bankers. These debts accelerated the collapsing process of the empire where the income did not actually meet the costs and the administration system was totally collapsed. Even though Abdülaziz tried to bring a system named Rüsûm-ı Sitte Administration in 1875 for the management of outer debts, it did not satisfy the creditors. This is noteworthy as a reason that accelerated Abdülaziz's being overthrown. Thus, much of the income of Ottoman Empire would be transferred to Düyun-u Umumiye Administration founded in the period of Abdülhamit and the financial bankruptcy of the empire would be carried out.

Abdülaziz is the only sultan who visited abroad apart from military expeditions. He visited Egypt and many states of the Ottoman country, went to France upon the invitation of Napoleon III and visited other European countries (England, Belgium, Germany and Austria-Hungary) throughout his journey. Among the important constructions built at the period of Abdülaziz, who was also interested in construction just like his predecessor Abdülmecit, we might mention Beylerbeyi and Çırağan Palaces as well as the Harbiye building, Aziziye Mosque in İstanbul-Maçka and Konya, Sadabad Mosque and again Valide Mosque at İstanbul-Aksaray.

Important developments and innovations occurred at Ottoman Empire during the period of Abdülaziz. Among the most important of these, construction of lighthouses in nearly all the shores to improve maritime business, founding of a modern firefighting organization instead of the traditional fire brigade, opening of the first high-schools in western sense (Galatasaray High School etc.), forming of Şura-i Devlet (State Council) and Divan-ı Muhasebat as the highest financial unit (Court of Accounts) can be mentioned. Opening of the schools of medicine, mining, forestry and reorganization of İstanbul University are all innovations that were carried out during his rule of 15 years. However, it is also a period when the public authority started to weaken both due to inability to provide financial discipline and riots that became wide-spread at some regions of the country especially at the Balkans. Crete, Wallachia and Moldavia were officially lost.

As a result, as we have stated above, Abdülaziz, who was overthrown with a palace intervention in the spring of 1876, could not accept this humiliation and committed suicide by cutting his wrists at Feriye palace where he was kept under supervision. However, there are also rumors that he did not commit suicide, but that he was killed by some clerks of the palace. The overthrown sultan who lost his life due to this event that took place shortly after Prince Murat V ascended the throne was buried in the tomb of his father Mahmut II at Divanyolu.

Sultan Abdülaziz, who lived a very colorful and rich seraglio life had 9 sons and 8 daughters.

SULTAN MURAT V

Murat V, who was the first son of his father Abdülmecit, was born in 1840 of Şevkefza Kadınefendi. He had a good education with the attention and care of both his father and his predecessor Sultan Abdülaziz and received lessons from the most famous scholars and tutors of his age. As the historians agree, he had a very soft, kind, delicate personality. He accompanied his uncle Sultan Abdülaziz in his travels to Egypt and Europe and gained valuable experience in the area of international relations.

However, Abdülaziz being taken down the throne and the events following that opened irreplaceable wounds in his delicate spirit.

He went through asevere mental depression and this condition went even worse. The death or murder of Abdülaziz and the rumors regarding it and Çerkez Hasan event that succeeded influenced the mental health of the young sultan negatively; Commander Çerkez Hasan who was the brother of a wife of Sultan Abdülaziz raided a council of ministers and killed Hüseyin Avni Paşa and diplomat Raşit Paşa. This event caused Murat V to lose his mind completely which was already weak at the time.

Even though he was treated by the best foreign doctors of the period, the result was not

Sultan Murat V

successful. He only mentioned the words "I do not want such a rule". As a result, on the 93rd day of inauguration, he descended the throne and his brother Abdülhamit II became the sultan. Murat V resided at Yıldız Palace during his brief reign.

The unsuccessful intervention attempt of Ali Suavi to take him to the power again a short while after he descended the throne made his anxiety and depression even worse. The sultan who relatively got better in the coming years spent the rest of his life at Çırağan Palace reading and taking care of his grandchildren. In August 1904, while he was 64, he died and was buried at a tomb near Yeni Mosque.

SULTAN ABDÜLHAMİT II

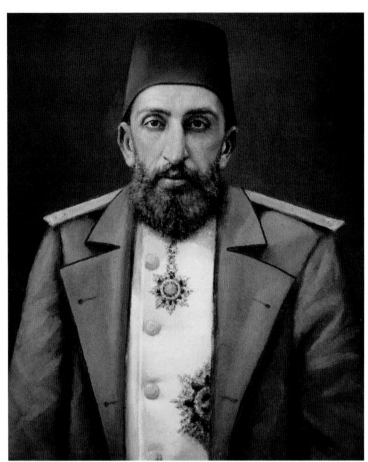

Sultan Abdülhamit II.

Abdülhamit II, who was the second male son of his father Abdülmecit, ascended the throne as the 34th sultan of Ottoman dynasty while he was 34 years old. First of all, he made Mithat Paşa his grand vizier, who was the hero and organizer of the overthrowing of his uncle Abdülhamit, and right afterwards announced constitutional monarchy as he pledged him.

Abdülhamit II, who witnessed the overthrowing of his uncle Sultan Abdülaziz and his brother Murat V, did not feel safe at Dolmabahçe Palace. Maybe, for this reason, he moved to the palace at Yıldız just in the 9th month of his inauguration and resided here continuously during the 33 years of his reign. Yıldız, having been transformed into a palace in the old style with separate buildings with the construction of new buildings became the symbol of the sultan. During these 33 years, Dolmabahçe Palace was only used for celebrations of religious fests and reception and dinners given on behalf of representatives of foreign countries.

In 1842, Abdülmecit ordered Kasr-ı Dilküşa to be built for his mother which represented the core of Yıldız Palace. Abdülaziz also ordered the great Mabeyn Mansion to be built and used this place especially during summers and when he organized wrestling activities. He had Malta Mansion and Çadır Mansion built in the part named as outer garden and eventually had Çit Summer House built adjacent to the central building.

The period when Abdülhamit II ascended the throne was when Ottoman Empire was in great distress and chaos. Public finance and treasure were in a condition of bankruptcy and in the meantime there were several riots in the Balkans. Abdülhamit approved the founding

28

of Düyun-u Umumiye (General Debts) administration in 1881 at a period when even the interests of the debts of the state could not be paid and declared the financial bankruptcy of Ottoman State and had to leave many income items to the administration of foreign creditors.

He was spiteful and had a secret agenda and he took action as soon as he found the opportunity. According to an article that he deliberately put in constitution (Kanun-u Esasi), he did not hesitate to send Mithat Paşa to exile even before the formation of the council because he considered him responsible for dethroning his uncle. This was an open sign that he would not tolerate Meclis-i Mebusan which was still closed at the time. Thus the Council was opened in March 1877, however, shortly after in April, the Great Russian war broke out and Sultan diffused Meclis-i Mebusan without a time limit not even a year after its opening in February of 1878.

The events following the war of 1877-1878 caused the Ottoman State to lose territory in the Balkans and recede. Abdülhamit and his administration did not have the power to supervise and guide these events. These unpleasant conditions led to new alliances. All these events encouraged the outside powers with various interests upon Ottoman Empire to put immense pressure to Abdülhamit II administration. Upon border violation by Greece to widen its land during the time of chaos and events at Crete, Turkish-Greek war broke out in 1897. At the beginning of this war, Turkish army was successful; however, due to exterior interventions once again, led by Russia this time, no permanent success was attained.

Abdülhamit who accelerated the police and investigator system after Çırağan Raid by Ali Suavi (attempt to re-throne Murat V) put into effect a new concept of administration where nearly all the powers were collected at the palace and in the hands of sultan who was also very repressive; this was called "autocracy period" and it continued until the declaration of the second Constitutional Monarchy. Such pressure accelerated the formation of a serious opposition at home and abroad. In the spring of 1908, a significant riot broke out in Roumelian states by some officers from Committee of Union and Progress against the administration of the Sultan and when it started to spread; Abdülhamit II had to put into effect the Constitution once again in July of the same year and called Meclis-i Mebusan to a meeting. However, with the increased provocations as well as the activities of the oppositions of Committee of Union and Progress in power, the riot named as 31st March Event started in the spring of 1909. Army of Action (Hareket) coming from Roumelia suppressed this riot through violence. A few days afterwards, Committee of Union and Progress took a council decision to dethrone Abdülhamit II for being responsible for this riot, and his period of 33 years ended with the declaration of the decision to him. The overthrown sultan was sent to exile in Saloniki. With the start of Balkan war in 1912, he was brought again to İstanbul and died in February of 1918. He was buried in the tomb of his grandfather Mahmut II in Divanyolu.

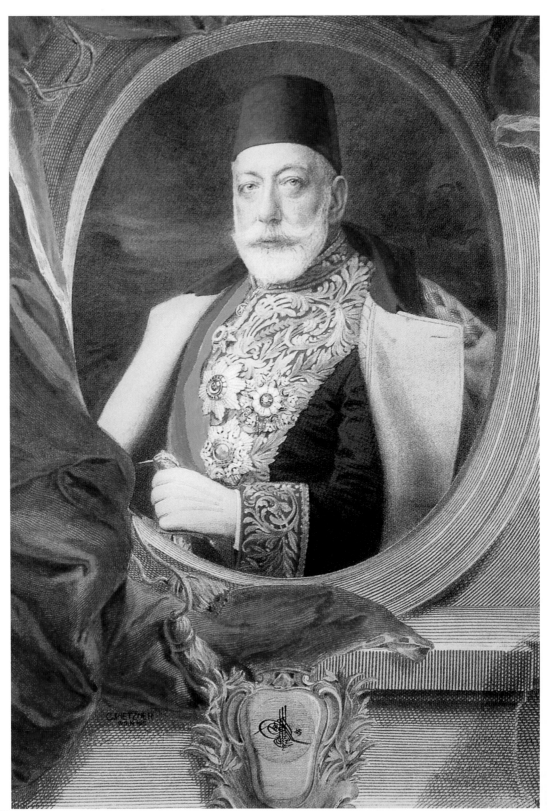

SULTAN MEHMET REŞAT V.

Mehmet Reşat, the third son of his father Abdülmecit, had 65 years of age and was an old and tired sultan when his brother Abdülhamit II was overthrown. He lived almost a prison life due to the worries of Abdülhamit II who witnessed his brother and uncle being overthrown, and was left ignorant of the developments in the world and the state affairs and could not gain any experience or information at all.

The 9 years of rule of Mehmet Reşat V passed under the influence and pressure of Committee of Union and Progress. During these 9 years, there was not even a case when the sultan was able to use his influence and power. He remained at Dolmabahçe palace like a puppet and did not interfere in anything. He only signed the papers brought before him and spent his years as such. The real power was in the hands of the three powerful men of Committee of Union and Progress; Enver Paşa, Talat Paşa and Cemal Paşa.

The first important event during the period of Mehmet Reşat V was the invasion of Libya that was named as the Tripoli state by Italy in 1911 and the war that started accordingly. The Ottoman officers such as Enver Bey and Mustafa Kemal, having a good cooperation with local powers, organized a strong resistance and blocked the Italian army at the shore preventing their success. However in 1912, at the end of the Great War that broke out in the Balkans the Uşi agreement was signed as a result of which Tripoli and the 12 Islands were lost. This also means the loss of the last territory of Ottoman Empire in Africa.

The Balkan War continued in two sections. In the first Balkan War, Bulgaria, Serbia, Montenegro and Greece defeated the Ottoman army and progressed until Çatalca near İstanbul. Starting with Saloniki and Edirne, nearly all the territory of Ottoman State was taken by this coalition of four. However, in the second Balkan War that took place among these countries, the Ottoman army used the opportunity to receive back some important territory. As a result of the intervention of European states, İstanbul agreement was entered and peace was attained through leaving Edirne and Kırklareli in Ottoman State accepting the Meriç River as the boundary.

In 1914, the war winds in Europe turned into a storm in a short while and as is known, the murder of crown prince of Austria-Hungary by a Serbian nationalist triggered the greatest war that human kind has ever seen. Enver Paşa, the powerful man of the triumvirate administering the Ottoman Empire was certain that the war would be won by the countries led by Germany and involved Ottoman Empire to the war with the hope and expectation of gaining maximum benefit from the great share. It was announced that the two German battle ships (Goeben -Yavuz- and Breslau -Midilli-) arriving in İstanbul escaping from British battleships were purchased by the Ottoman Empire. However, these two battleships remained under the rule of German captain, officers and sailors and soon, they began to bomb the cities of Russia on Black Sea shores and especially Odesa and declared war actively and thus Ottoman Empire entered the World War I.

While these vital decisions were taken and applied, Enver Paşa and other managers of Committee of Union and Progress did not even have the decency to consult Mehmet Reşat V. The old and tired sultan had to watch all these tragic developments from outside like a strager.

As is known, Turkish-Ottoman armies who had to fight at many different battlefields especially the Caucasus and Dardanelles in the World War I became quite exhausted in the fourth year of the war. The bad news that arrived the palace caused Mehmet Reşat who was 74 years old at the time (1918) to be exhausted and he died of heart failure in July. He was buried in the tomb that he reserved in Eyüp.

SULTAN MEHMET VAHDETTİN VI

Mehmet Vahdettin, the fourth son of his father Abdülmecit, was 57 years old when he ascended the throne upon the death of his brother. Until 1922, the date he left the throne and the capital, he lived at Dolmabahçe Palace.

After the onset of the World War I, Vahdettin visited Germany upon invitation when he was the prince and Mustafa Kemal participated in this travel as an aide. It is known that while preparing for the Indepence War, Mustafa Kemal expected support from Vahdettin due to this acquaintance but that the Sultan did not meet these expectations.

When Vahdettin ascended the throne, the result of the war was then obvious. Thus, in the end of October of the same year, in a British battleship at Mondros Port of Limni Island, a ceasefire was signed ending the armed conflict for Ottoman State. Vahdettin, the palace and the statesmen examined the text of the agreement and presented it to signature and they perceived that it meant the actual end of Ottoman State. However, they did not resist or try to lighten the conditions; they approved it without any opposition. Afterwards, Mustafa Kemal would say that this attitude of Vahdettin was the start of a betrayal process.

The total surrender and submission attitude of Sultan and İstanbul government towards the winners of the war led to even stronger riots in Anatolia. Vahdettin believed that the Anatolian revolution led by Mustafa Kemal formed a great danger to his throne. The palace did not hesitate to approve the decisions of military commission positioning the "nationalist" leaders of Ankara administration fighting for the nation against the foreign powers for independence of the nation under the penalty of death. He would also sign the Treaty of Sevres in July of the same year that was discussed and written in San Remo conference in April 1920 destroying Ottoman State.

After the Turkish army won the great victory at the end of national struggle and entered İstanbul, Vahdettin thought that his life was in danger and applied to commandment of invading armies demanding shelter from England. When it was approved, on 17th, November 1922 he boarded on Malaya battleship of England and left İstanbul, Dolmabahçe palace and his throne which already had lost its meaning, and left Turkey. He stayed at Malta Island for a while, went to Hejaz and returned to Italy. He lived in San Remo city until his death in May 1926.

With the escape of Vahdettin Mehmet VI, the Ottoman dynasty came to an end legally and effectively. However, the future of caliphate title owned by Ottoman dynasty with the conquest of Egypt by Yavuz Sultan Selim kept its uncertainty. Ankara government brought Abdülmecit Efendi to this rank who did not have an open attitude against National Struggle even supported it. The last guest of Dolmabahçe Palace from the dynasty was this last caliph.

CALIPH ABDÜLMECİT

Abdülmecit Efendi was born in 1868 as the son of Sultan Abdülaziz. In 1922, when Vahdettin escaped from the country, he was 54 years old. During the period of Sultan Abdülhamit II, he was also compelled to a closed life spending these years especially with drawing. He was a talented painter, calligrapher and even an interesting author in his own limits. He had a prose work named "Memories" which is nearly 12 volumes including very interesting information.

Upon the annulment of sultanate and the last sultan escaping abroad, he was chosen as a caliph by Turkish Grand National Assembly. However, this became a purely symbolic title without any power of sultanate rule. The regulation sent by Ankara Government stated that he would use no other title than the Caliph of the Muslims ("Halife-i Müslimin"). However, Abdülmecit could not really agree to this condition. During this period of 15 years, he resided at Dolmabahçe Palace, attempted to act like a sultan sometimes and disturbed Ankara Government and Atatürk. Eventually, Turkish Grand National Assembly removed the title of caliphate (March 3, 1924) and decided that all the members of Ottoman dynasty be sent abroad. Upon this, Abdülmecit had to leave the country, went to Switzerland and than France and died in Paris in 1944. His tomb is in Medina.

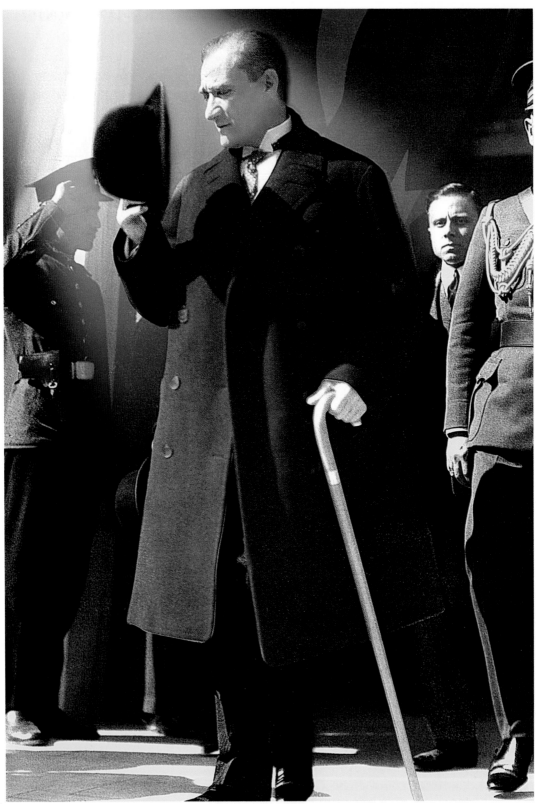

THE PALACE ADMINISTRATION TRANSFER TO TURKISH GRAND NATIONAL ASSEMBLY AND ATATÜRK

When Ottoman dynasty was sent abroad, the ownership and administration of Dolmabahçe Palace was transferred to Turkish Grand National Assembly.

Atatürk did not come to İstanbul for years after İstanbul was saved from foreign invaders and the dynasty was sent abroad. His first visit was in 1927 and he was welcomed at the Dolmabahçe Palace. In his other visits, if we accept the days he spent at the summer mansion as exceptional, he always resided at this palace. During the days until his death, he accepted and welcomed the foreign statesmen and guests visiting İstanbul at Dolmabahçe. Among the most famous of them, Iranian Shah Rıza Pehlevi, Iraqi King Faysal, Jordanian King Abdullah, Afghanistani King Amanullah Han, British King Edward VIII and Yugoslavian King Alexandre can be mentioned.

The palace was opened to public for the first time after its construction during the period of Atatürk in 1937 upon his order. This was a unique event in history. It can be accepted as the beginning of the process which turned the palace into a museum.

Atatürk, who spent the last months and days at this palace, closed his eyes here on life on November 10th, 1938 here.

Between 1938-1950, President İsmet İnönü stayed at this palace during his visits to İstanbul. When Celal Bayar was the prime minister and president (1937-1938 and 1950-1960), it was used only during the receptions, feasts and meetings held for the honor of official guests. Since 1964, it has been serving Turkish tourism as one of the most important museums of İstanbul and Turkey.

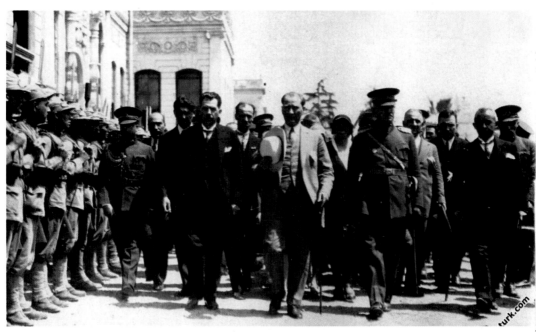

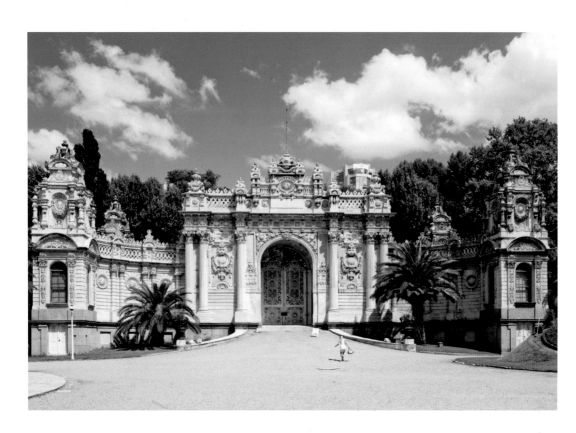

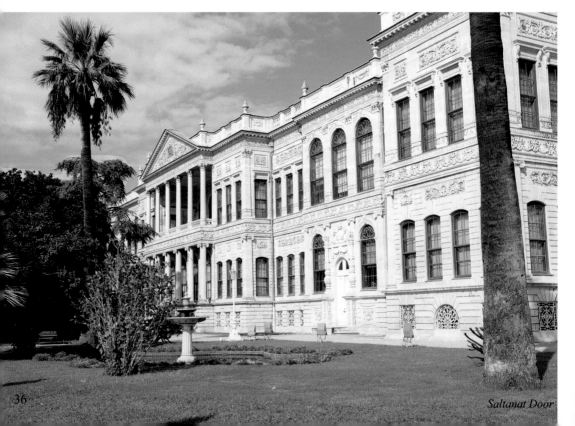

Saltanat Door

Section 6
SECTIONS OF THE PALACE

As we have stated above (III), Dolmabahçe Palace consists of three sections (Mabeyn-i Humayun, Muayede lounge and Seraglio) and auxiliary buildings where all the needs of the people living in the palace were met. These sections are:

a) Doors

The doors of the palace, especially Saltanat Door and Treasury Door, are extremely beautiful structures worth special attention. Apart from these two, the others are Valide Door, Harem Door, Bendegan Door and Kuşluk Doors and each one of them is special. There are also five seaside doors.

Saltanat Door and Treasury Door are extremely beautiful doors that separate from other doors with their art structure and ornamentation. Among the doors that give passage to the

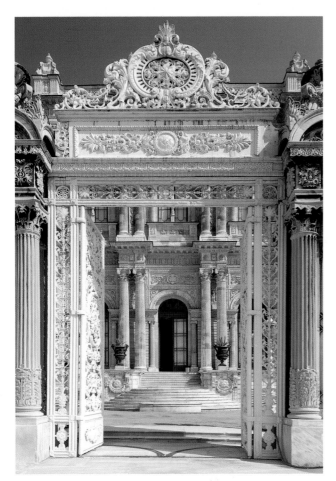

ones coming from the seaside, the one in front of Muayede room is called the Saltanat Sea Door. The one close to Mabeyn-i Humayun is named as Vizier Port Door. Apart from these there are three more doors named as Yalı Doors.

For visiting the palace, entrance and exit is made through the Treasury Door. Because the cars are left to the parking lot surrounding the Clock Tower, the visitors generally leave without seeing Saltanat Door. For this reason, before returning to the cars, we suggest that you take a joyful walk among the walls of the palace for a few hundred meters and see this excellent door.

Seaside mansion door before Muayede Lounge

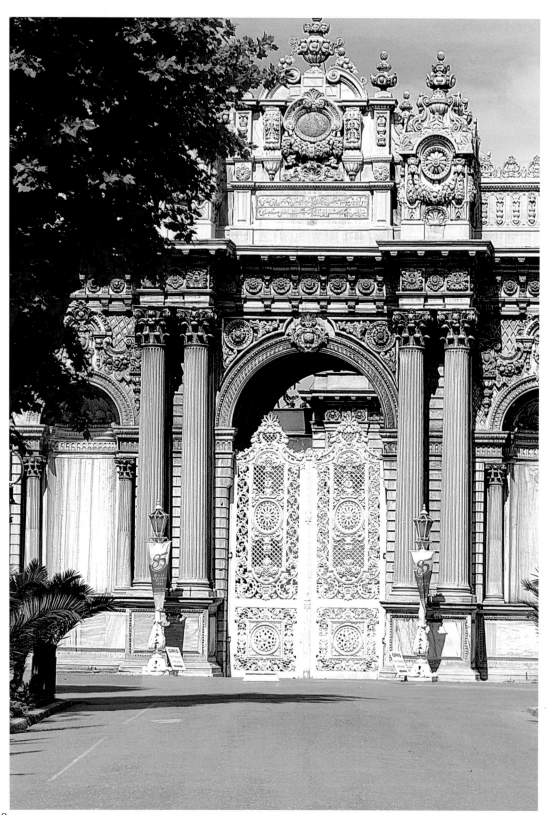

Saltanat Door

b) Gardens

Dolmabahçe palace is organized beautifully, spacious and surrounded with green gardens. In these gardens, there are some features that are seen in the gardening order of the palaces in Western countries. The most important reason for this is claimed to be the people responsible of the garden in the last phase of the construction of the palace and the period afterwards were brought from Europe (Germany). As this is important in garden organization, it would be better to evaluate this issue within the Western influence that is dominant in the architecture of the palace.

The most important and the most magnificent of the gardens is the Great Garden with the Pool between Treasury Door and Mabeyn building. Apart from the grass and flower pools, rare trees brought from different countries in the world complete the beauty of this garden. The ornamented swan sculpture in the middle of the large pool acts as a fountain.

The rest of this garden is located in front of the palace at the part overlooking the sea. In the front garden where the same ornament order is dominant as in the Great Garden with Pool, there are two smaller pools.

In the land side of Mabeyn building, there is Kuşluk Garden that carries pretty different features from the previous ones with its organization and ornamentation and it is a pretty

Hasbahçe

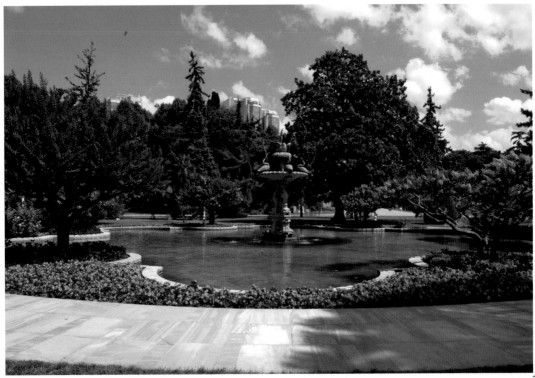

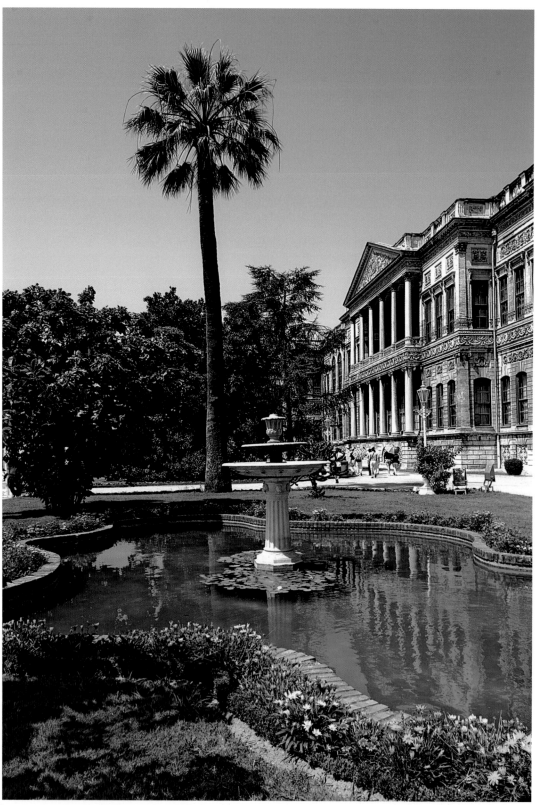

beautiful example of Turkish garden architecture. Kuşluk building and Kuşluk Mansion that gives its name to the garden, containing birds with different features such as parrot types, pheasants, peacocks and lovebirds are also in this garden that has a dimmer and relaxing atmosphere.

For those who will make a complete tour of the palace, it is suggested that they visit the garden of the Harem section. Clock Museum that is reached actually via this garden located just next to it includes a splendid collection. This building was organized as Inner Treasury during the time when the palace was used by the Dynasty.

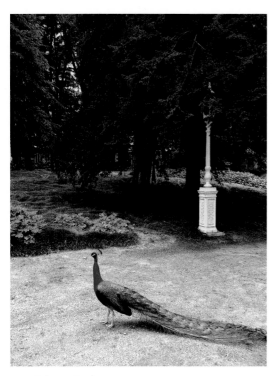

Kuşluk Garden

View from the garden

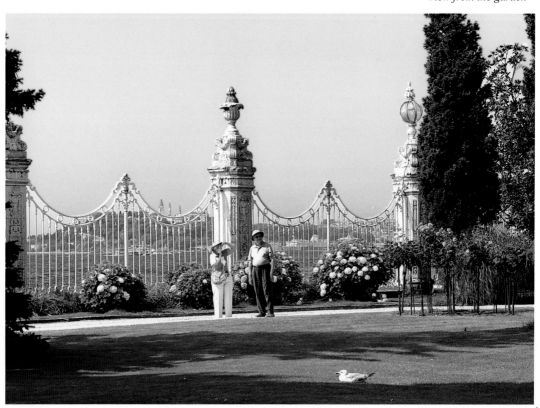

Section 7

VISITING THE PALACE

The tour of Dolmabahçe Palace is started through the entrance named Treasury Door. We suggest the visitors to spare some time to Dolmabahçe Mosque that has the thinnest minaret in the world and Clock Tower before entering the palace or during exit. Besides, as we have stated when mentioning the doors of the palace above, before or after the palace visit, Saltanat Door shall be seen with a short trip.

a)Mabeyn-i Humayun building

When the palace is reached through the garden with Great Pool, Mabeyn-i Humayun, or in short the Mabeyn building which is a totally functional but very elegant building is entered after ascending some elegant stairs. This is the place the sultan used as an office. It is the location where the important high officials of the state as well as the embassies of foreign countries could meet and visit the sultan.

The entrance location that meets the people entering the building is named as Medhal Lounge (meaning including, entering). The Room with Two Facades (Zülveçheyn room) located on the upper floor that is ascended with very elegant crystal stairs provides the passage to Hünkar Room named as Inner Mabeyn. Again, inside this building, Sefirler room (Süfera, diplomats) has a magnificent beauty and a very rich decoration in order to influence the for-

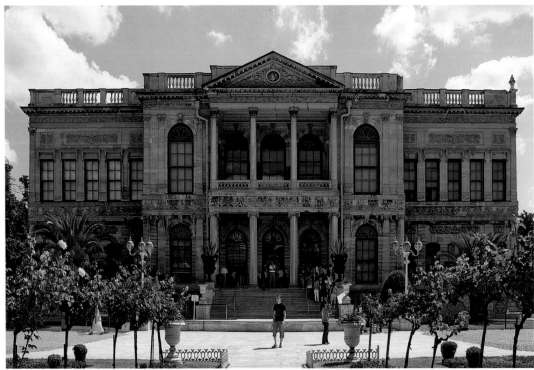

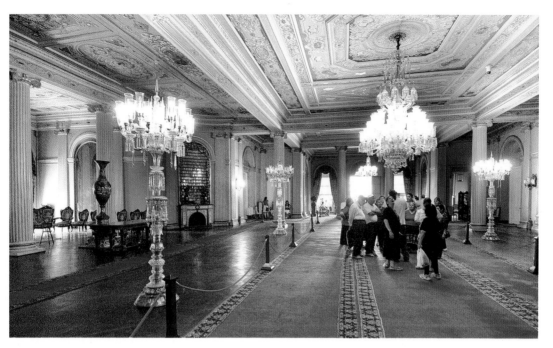

Entrance Room (Medhal Room)

eign guests. The Red Room entered after passing from this room where foreign guests meet the sultan is one of the most beautiful locations of Mabeyn building.

Entrance Room (Medhal Room)

The local and foreign visitors who come to meet the sultan or the palace officials of high rank entered the palace from this room. Also today, the first step of those who come to visit the palace is from here. The sultans also used this room and its door for official purposes in order to participate in activities such as Friday greetings, religious feasts or the Kadir legion. It is illuminated with a British crystal chandelier with 60 arms. In the palace, there are 36 chandeliers which are the same or similar to this one. In the lounge, two small chandeliers made up of Baccarat crystal draw attention immediately and there are two more standing chandeliers with the same quality. In the two sides of the room, there are studies used by the grand vizier (prime minister) and other ministers. The ceiling of the room is ornamented by gilding and pencil work. The fireplaces for heating purposes also have a very rich ornamentation. The porcelain plates and trimmed crystals in the vaulted head pieces, flower vases, symbols of fertility and magnificent crowns are marvelous. The Sevres and Chinese bowls over these fire places, besides the local (Yıldız Porcelain) column vases are among the most beautiful examples of their kind with their extraordinarily beauty and ornamentation. It should be noted that the carpets in the main location and in the adjacent rooms are the products of Hereke workshops. The dominant color in the curtains and seating groups is royal red also woven in Hereke.

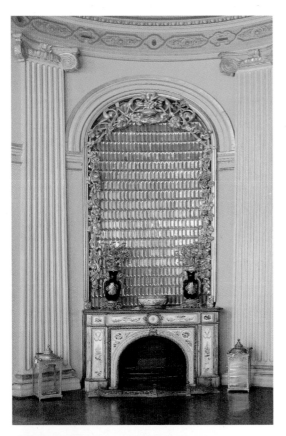

The columns in Ionian order show the ceiling higher than it is and give the room a spacious effect. All these architectural applications and ornamentations carried the purpose of impressing the guests who came to the palace. Again, on both sides of the lounge, two tables ornamented with the signature of Abdülmecit are striking. The signature over the door opening to the stairs with crystal stairs symbolizes the passage to the royalty.

This lounge was also used in Atatürk period for Language Assembly and similar international activities.

Vizier and Sürre rooms

There is a room in the sea part compared to entrance (Medhal) Lounge that the grand viziers used when coming to the palace. Right across it, on the garden side,

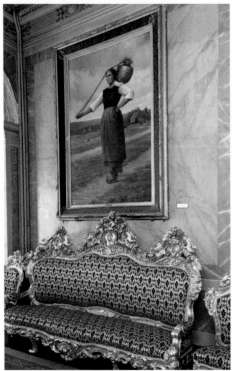

there is a room where the gifts and gold sent to Hejaz every year with "Sürre legion" were packaged and placed in bags.

Writing Office

During the palace visit, when you progress from the right/front side door instead of the stairs, you arrive at the Lounge with China known as the Writing Office. This place served as some sort of a waiting room. The sofa in the middle of the lounge and especially the armchairs in the balcony carry functional features in order to provide the comfort of the guests. The most striking elements of this lounge are the paintings on the walls. Ernst (fire at Paris Opera) on the left wall and Ussi (Sürre legion) on the right wall shall be mentioned among the most valuable pieces of the palace.

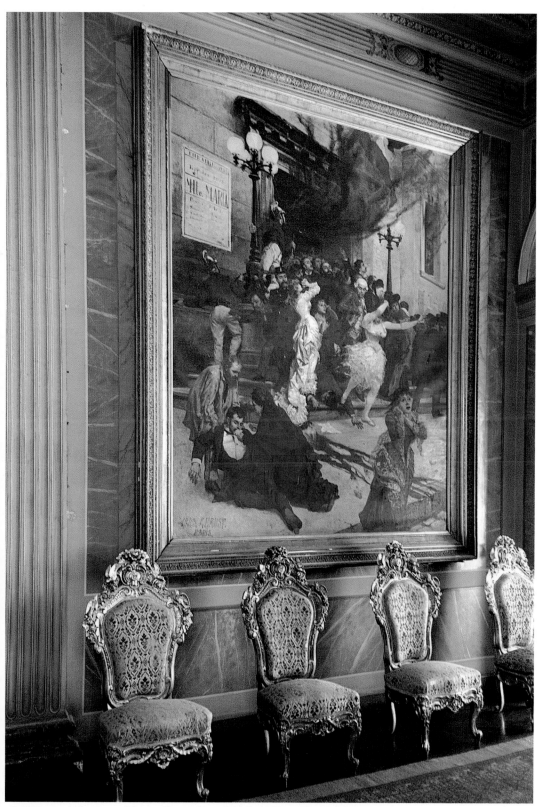

Painting with the theme "Opera Fire at Paris" by Ernst located in the Writing Room   45

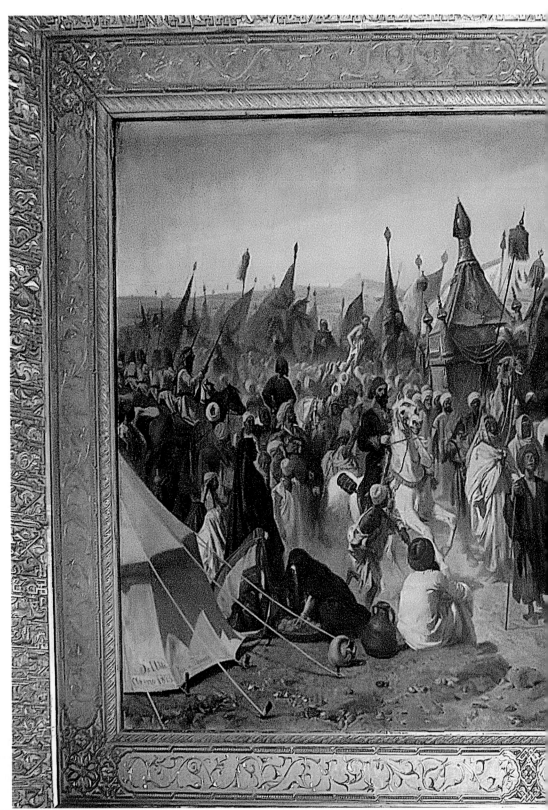

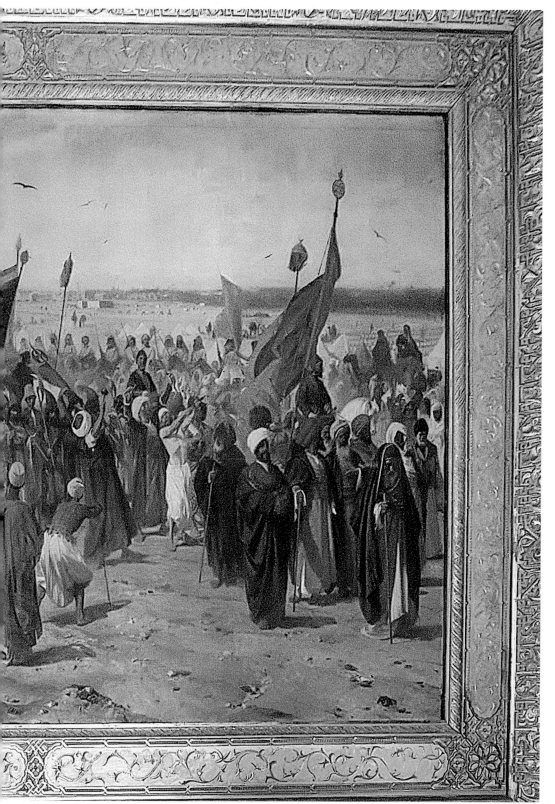

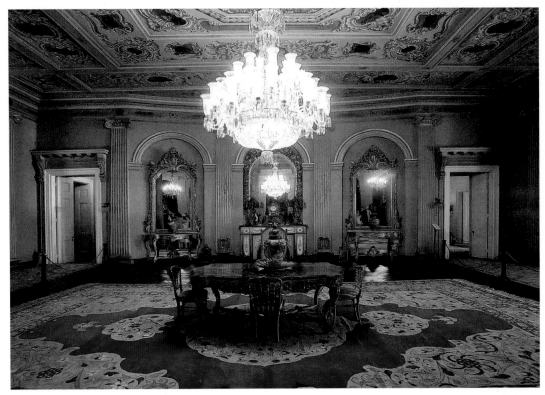

Passenger Lounge

Passenger Lounge

The wide room that is entered through the writing office is named as Passenger Lounge and was used for daily entrance and exit to the palace. The door on the seaside is opened to the pier and the door right across this was used while going to Saltanat Door. This lounge with its decoration carries an integrated style with Medhal Lounge and Writing Office. The carpet in the lounge has Hereke medallion style and is among the most beautiful examples of its kind. We shall say the same thing for the main chandelier and the column chandeliers on the sides used for the illumination of the lounge. The golden gilded mirrors and two way commodes give a last impression before going outside and the Baccarat vases ornamenting them are among its most beautiful examples.

Mosque and resting room

On the left front side of Passenger Lounge, there is first the resting and preparation for worship rooms and just next to it, there is the Mosque used by both the guests and the high officials of the palace. Because there is no running water in the location of the Mosque, the watering can and basins for those preparing for namaz prayer are displayed in resting room.

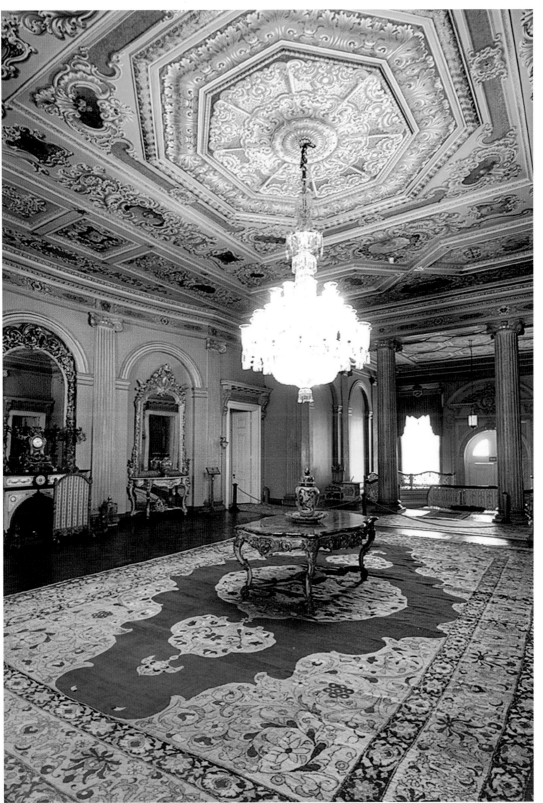

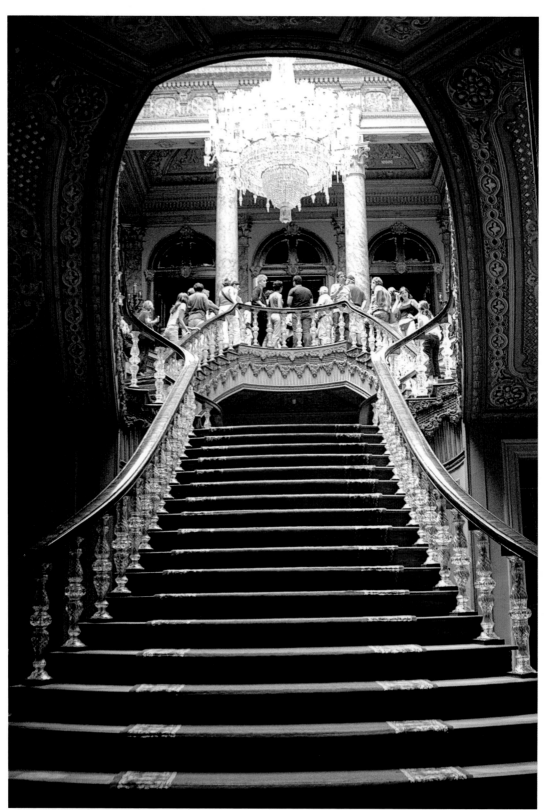

Conflicting with the elegant Hereke carpet and a small Horasan carpet in the mosque, the floor of the resting room is covered with machine carpet. The chandelier of the mosque is a unique and elegant piece that carries the sign of Murano.

Passage to Upper Floor

After visiting the mosque, one can ascend the upper floor via the famous crystal stairs. The location is first of all illuminated with the glass cover on its ceiling. However, there is a gorgeous chandelier over the middle of the stairs. In the middle section, these magnificent stairs combined to the floor of upstairs by separating into two and thus four contribute to the local brightness and brilliance effect. Progressing to the direction of entrance of the palace

Crystal Stairs

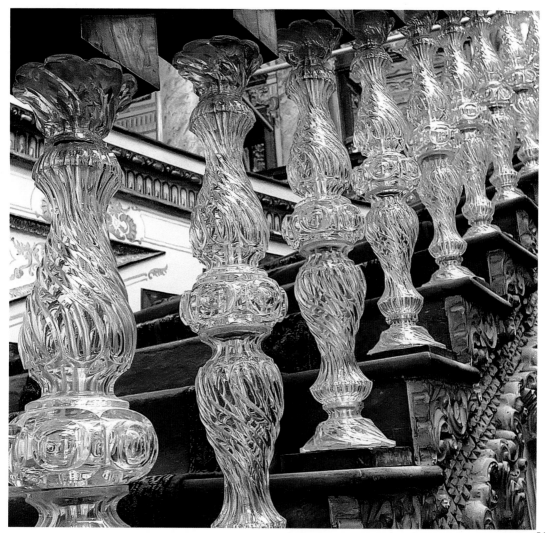

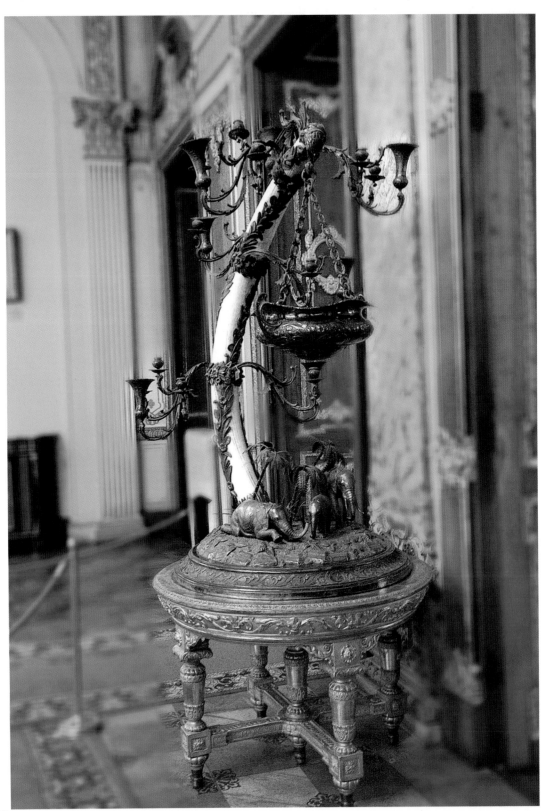

while ascending the stairs, there is the door of Sefirler Lounge. On both sides of this door, there are ivory chandeliers which are extraordinarily beautiful and important pieces sent from Arabia (Hejaz state) as a present to the palace. The decoration of the location is enriched with thurible, Far-East vases, silver flower beds, clocks and of course beautiful and magnificent paintings on the walls.

Ivory chandeliers   *Crystal Stairs and chandelier*

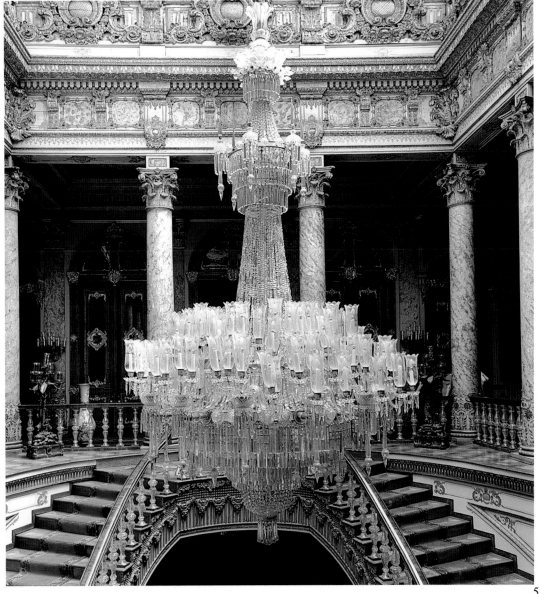

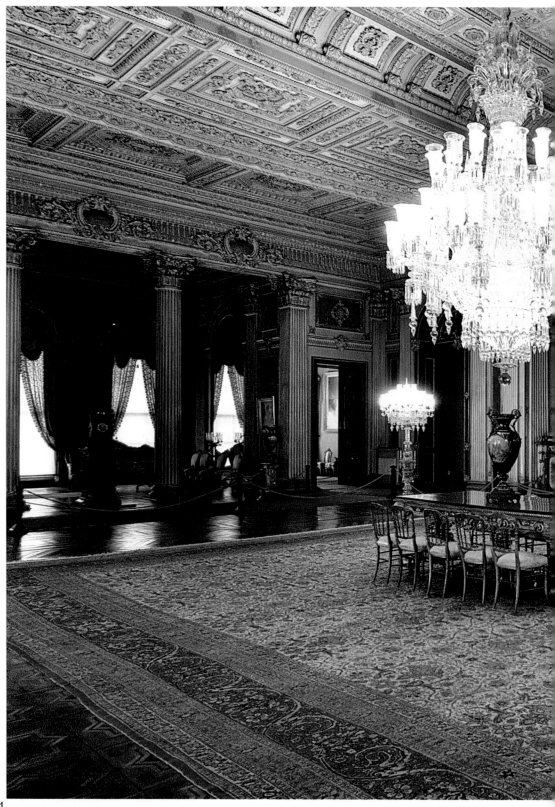

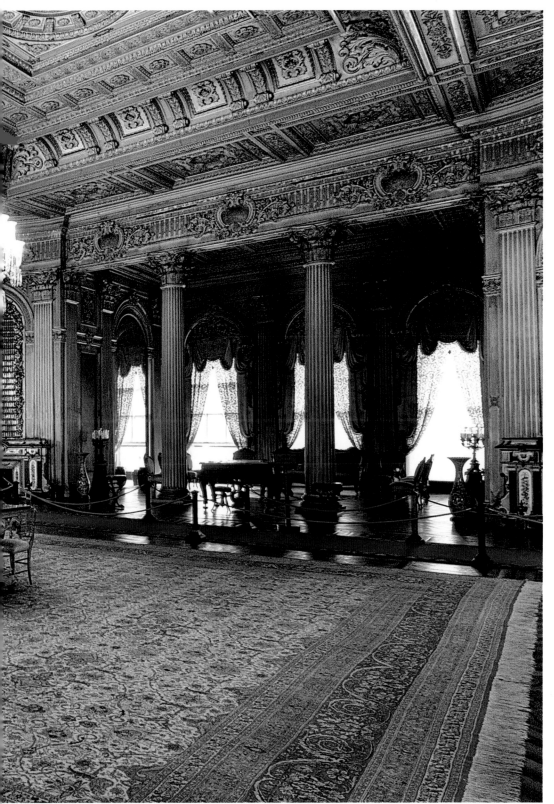

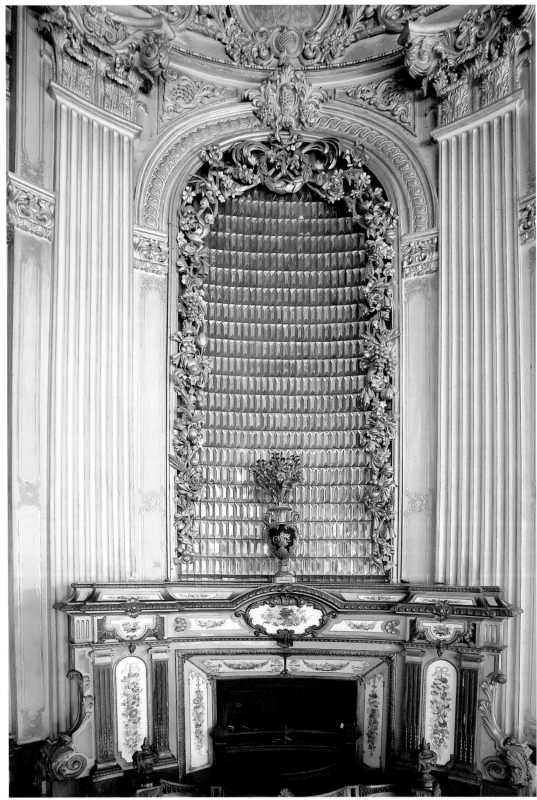

Mabeyn Lounge or Ambassadors (Süfera) Lounge

Mabeyn Lounge located right above the entrance lounge to the palace (Medhal Lounge) or Embassy Lounge – its other name used rarely – draws attention with its uniquely rich decoration and valuable and beautiful items. When entered to the parlour, one would directly look at the magnificent chandelier that is made of Baccarat crystals and the extraordinary beauty of the ceiling: This ceiling decorated by the most famous Italian and French artists of the period enriched with golden gild leaves all viewers in astonishment.

The representatives of foreign countries visiting the sultan according to their appointment were taken to this lounge first. It would be correct to assume that these diplomats who were actually very excited in their first visit to present their letters of trust were very much impressed before the glory of this lounge. The glorious fire places ornamented with porcelain and crystals, the high chandeliers located in the four corners of the lounge and giant vase of Yıldız Porcelain, Tebriz and Hereke carpets on the floor of the lounge, coffee tables with silver legs, again silver braziers and ornamented seating groups as well as the white bear fur which is a gift of the Russian Tsar increase this effect even more.

Mabeyn Lounge or Ambassadors (Süfera) Lounge

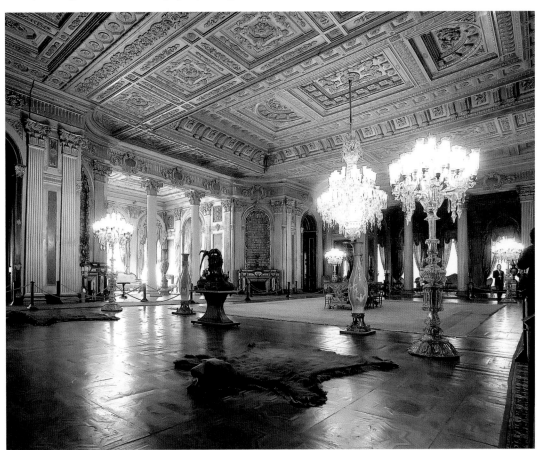

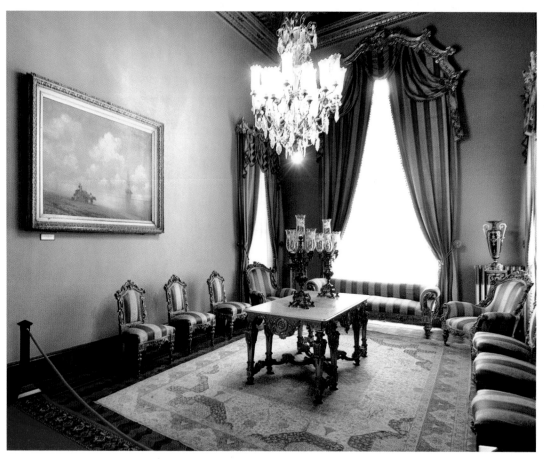

Translator Room

Translators and ambassadors rooms

These rooms, smaller in comparison with the lounges, are completely functional but still draw attention with their ornamented decoration. The walls are ornamented with very valuable painters of Ayvazovski, Zonaro, Rocholl and other painters, the ground is covered with thin and elegant Hereke carpets and the room is decorated with high clocks, mirrors with golden gild and commodes.

Waiting room

This room which is larger and pretty bright compared to Translation and Embassy rooms is decorated with special attention as the last location the diplomats were taken before being brought in front of the Sultan. The Sevres porcelain over the elegant table ornamenting the space has a striking beauty. The view that can be seen from 11 windows through wall ornamentation and curtains give a spacious and ornamented look to the room. Here, we have to specify the beauties of crystal chandelier and the very rich ceiling and veil ornamentation.

Acceptance Lounge

The foreign diplomats who passed from these rooms and phases were accepted by the Sultan in this room. In the curtains made of heavy cloth woven in Hereke ateliers and again in the seating places, it is seen that royal red is used. The decoration of the walls and the ceiling is very glorious. The central chandelier in this room presents a very impressive view. The fireplaces ornamented with crystals and the coffee tables with enamels have a striking beauty. On the floor, there is a very elegant Iranian carpet. This lounge has a special importance because it witnessed many bitter events of the last period of Ottoman history. The bitter meetings that the last Sultan Vahdettin Mehmet VI had with the diplomats of the countries who won the World War I and especially the ones he made with the commanders of occupation power due to the independence struggle in Anatolia were all carried out in this room...

Waiting room

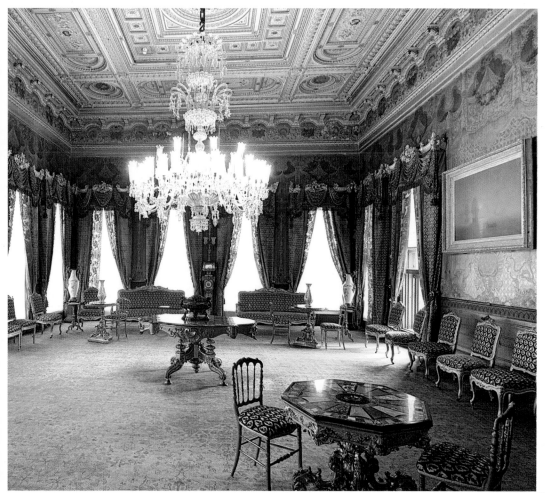

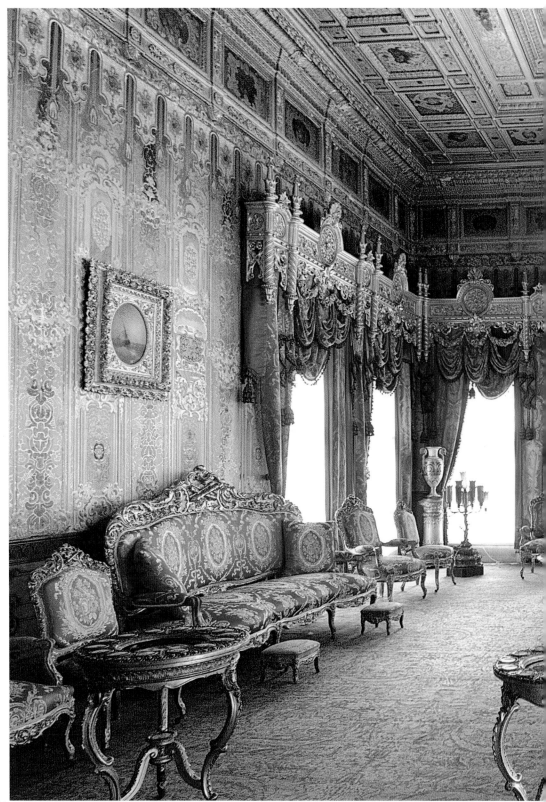

Acceptance Lounge

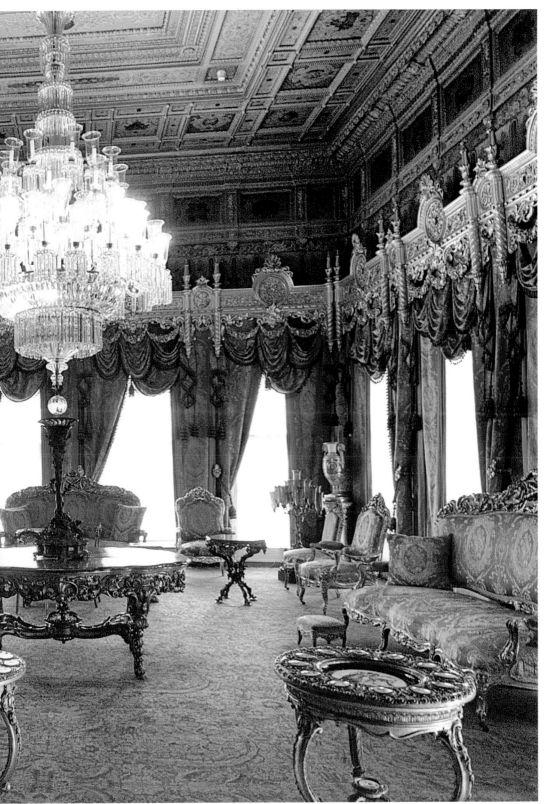

Porphyry room

One of the two rooms that the sultan sometimes used for his private meetings, related to the lower floor with separate and special stairs is named as Porphyry Room because of the different quality of the green colored porphyry stone used on its walls. These two rooms can not be visited in the regular palace visits due to the entrance-exit difficulties it has, but can be seen with a special permission given to special guests.

***

At the side of the sea, a small room used especially in meetings of two and the Relic Room (Sakal-ı Şerif room) across it on the garden side are among the parts of the palace worth seeing at this part. Crown prince location again located on the sea part consisting of two telescopic rooms has an impressive view with its decoration and beauty. Also the small room named as Green Room due to the colors in its decoration on the sea part is worth seeing for the elegant silk Hereke carpet and the paintings of Italian Pasini.

In the platform seen after exiting from Mabeyn (Süfera) Lounge and arriving in the middle

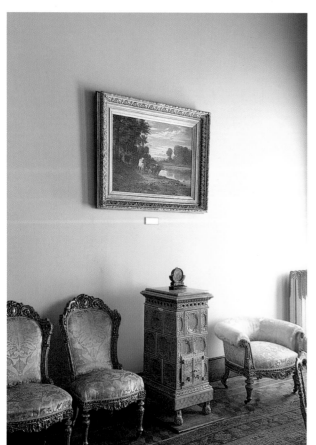

location draws the attention of the visitors with the most beautiful crystal chandeliers and three clocks with ornamentation. The elegance of the silver flower beds displayed in the section overlooking the garden creates a striking effect. In the records of the palace, it is seen that these flower beds were brought from India.

Right after one passes from the glass screen, the beautiful wooden craftsmanship over the floor is worth seeing. The Syrian (Damascus) handmade cupboard and the Far-Eastern (China) vases placed over them on a silver base are among the most beautiful types of its kind.

***

The room with dual meetings

The Lounge with Two Sides(Zülveçheyn Lounge)

This location which is the passage location from inner mabeyn to outer mabeyn is among the most beautiful rooms of Mabeyn section with the rich but modest decoration. The beautiful floor pavement starting right outside, the parquet gets even more beautiful and continues in this room. It is known that in this room that the sultans frequently used for different purposes, wedding ceremonies were held, mevlid was read in Ramadan and dinners were given for the representatives of foreign countries. This room also bears a special importance as a room that the Seraglio women can use in Mabeyn building. The decoration dominated with the color green has more plain lines and features. However, this lounge also carries the feature of being a relaxing and elegant location of the palace with its crystal fireplace, cupboard on both sides with pearl inlaid, a very beautiful chandelier, green varnished piano and elegant seating groups.

The Lounge with Two Sides (Zülveçheyn Lounge)

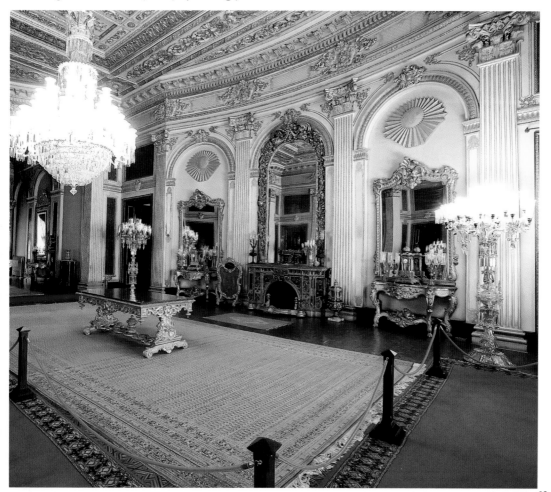

The Study of the Sultan, the White Room and the Library

When you proceed from the Lounge with Two Sides from the seaside, you arrive first of all at the library and then the White Room from the library. The library was formed by the last caliph Abdülmecit who was extremely interested in reading and who had his own personal book collection. The large room entered through here is called White Room and is a functional location the sultans used for studying sometimes. A glorious china stove that is located in this room is a very beautiful and interesting example of its kind. The decision of Turkish Grand National Assembly regarding sending Ottoman Dynasty abroad was announced to the last caliph, Abdülmecit in this room. After this announcement, the family left the country with a special train within four hours. Besides this, the small room is a study that is preferred by some residents of the palace, especially Sultan Mehmet Reşat. It is known that this sultan examined the official papers presented to him for signing or transferring in this room. This room is not included in the regular visit program due to the difficulty in its entrance and exit.

Music room

The first location in the left end of the lounge with two sides (Zülveçheyn) is named the music room. The sons and daughters of the sultans took music lessons in this room. In the decoration of the room, attention was given to functionality and comfortable armchairs de-

fined as berger armchair and chairs ornamented with motifs are placed. Various paintings ornament the walls. This room where there is also a beautiful china stove is completed by a very beautiful piano.

Hammam

One of the most beautiful sultan hammams of six in the palace is located at the end of Mabeyn section. The entrance part was also used as a resting room. In this room, there is one of the most beautiful chandeliers of the palace. This is a very rare Murano chandelier. The blue color lanterns of the elegant and beautiful wall-lights made of Bohemian crystals is worth seeing. The walls and the ground of the heating room are covered with a special marble brought from Egypt. This marble, the light of which is very transparent is one of the rarest examples of its kind.

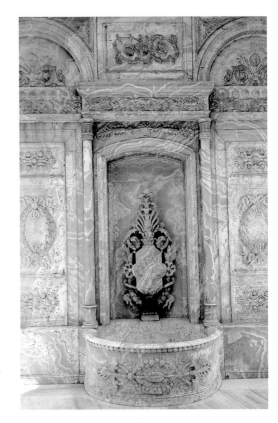

Hammam

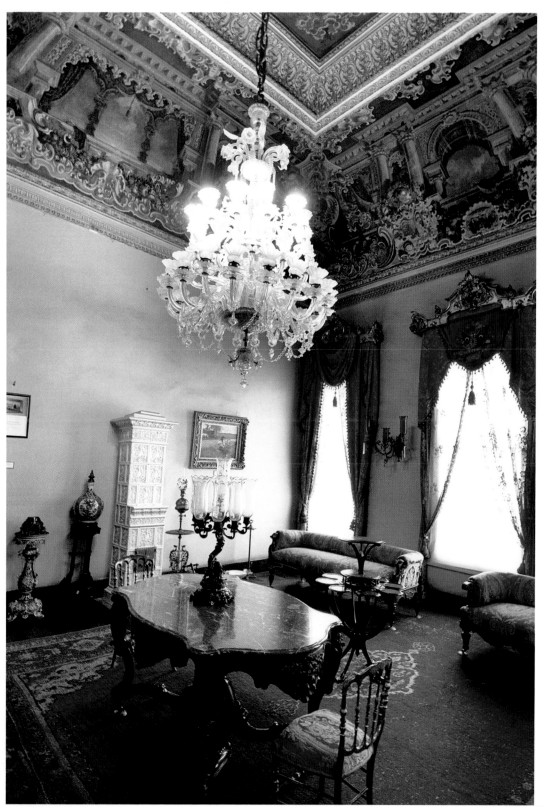

Resting room of Hünkar Hamam

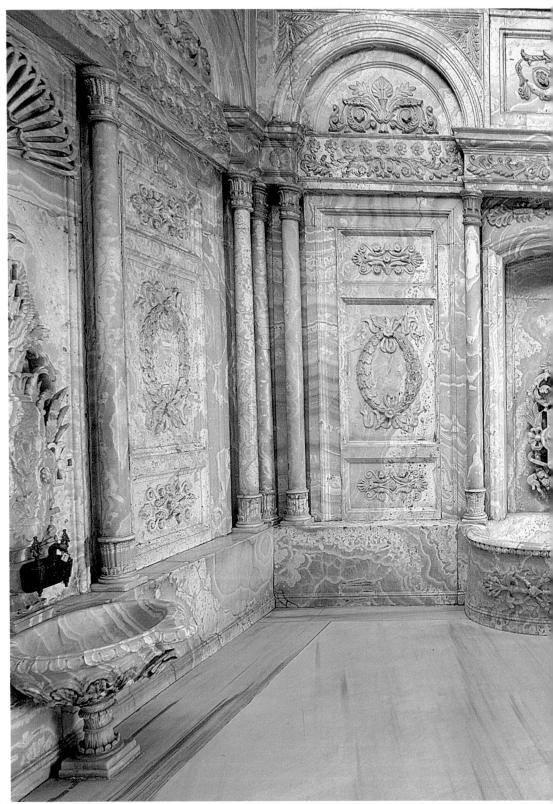

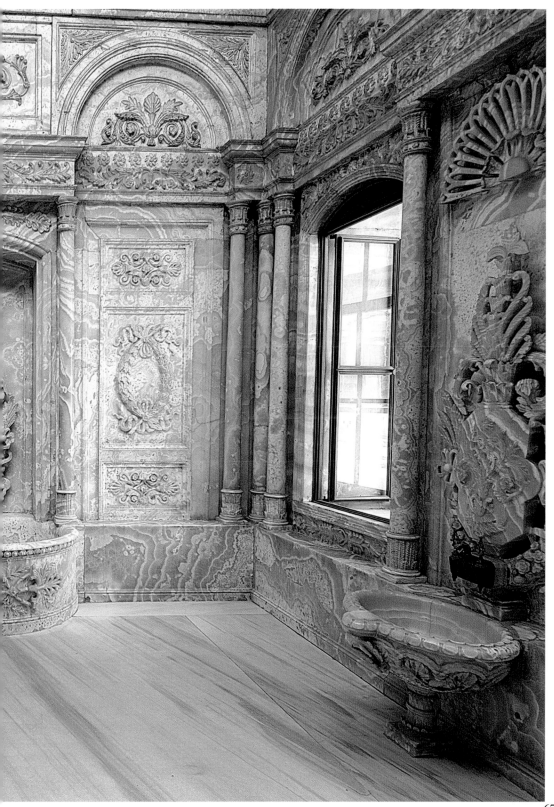

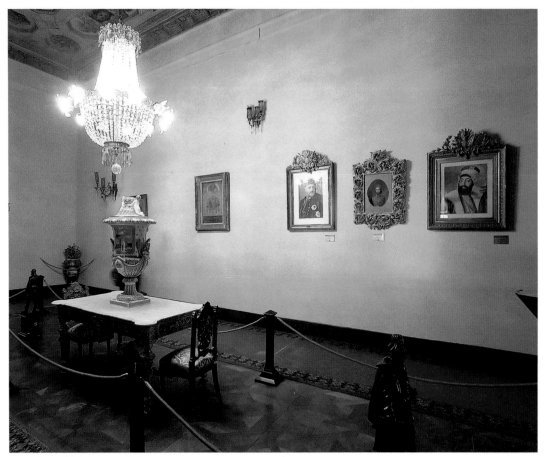

Lounge of Memories

The last rooms of Mabeyn building

Right across sultan's hammam and at the beginning of the passage corridor towards Seraglio section, there is a large room named Memories Room. The crystal chandelier made with delicate craftsmanship and the Meissen vase over the small table in the middle draws attention. On the walls of this room, there are paintings of Abdülaziz and Mehmet Reşat, the two of the four sons of Mahmut II, the father of Sultan Abdülmecit as well as emblems that belong to the dynasty. Through the stairs that give passage to Muayede lounge, there are photographs and paintings sent as presents from many important foreigners.

Before continuing with the explanation of Muayede lounge, let's mention finally an inner room near the music room. On the walls of this inner room that is ornamented by a perfect Hereke carpet woven skillfully in color pink as well as a gorgeous commode with mirror and a crystal chandelier, the large painting of "Dethroning of Abdülhamit" made by Caliph Abdülmecit is extremely interesting.

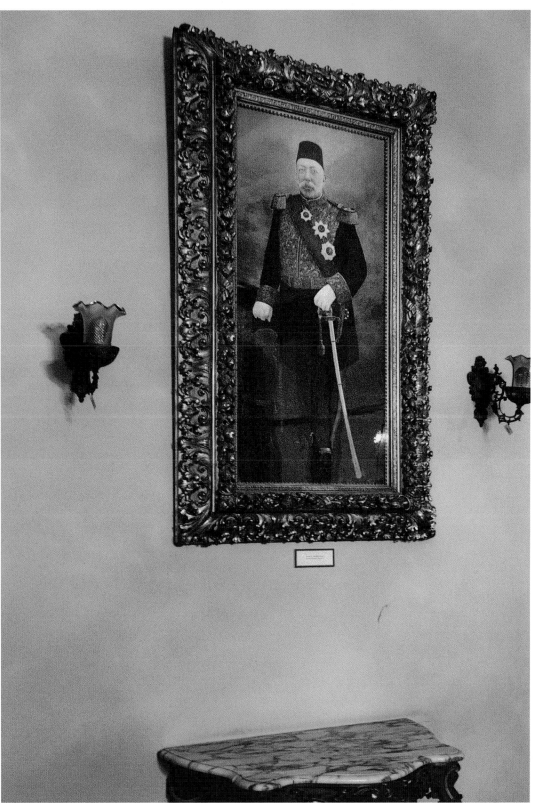

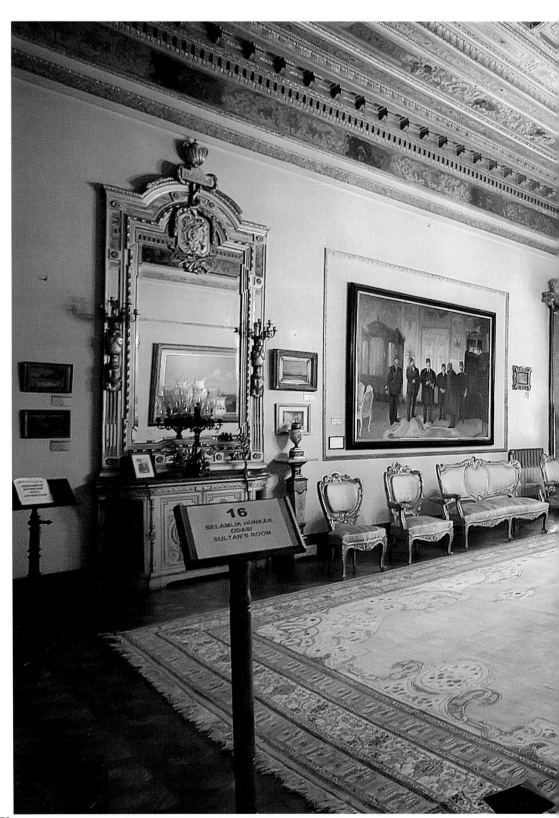

The room with the painting "De-throning of Abdülhamit"

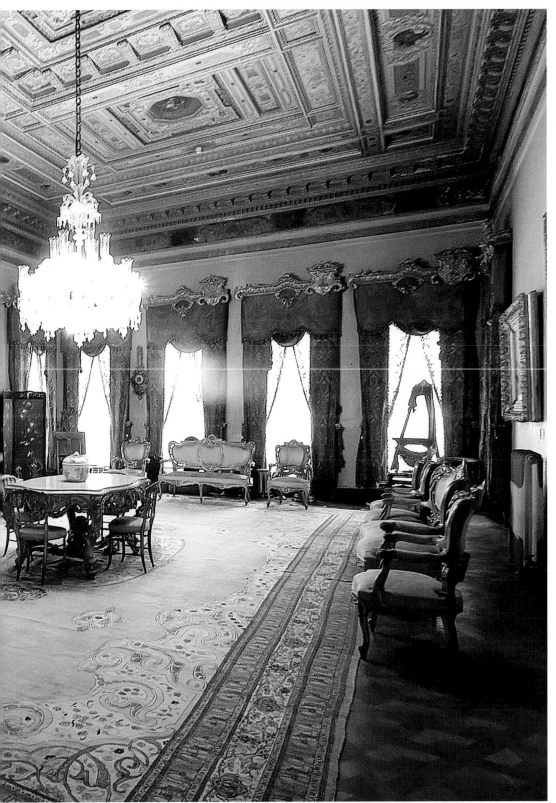

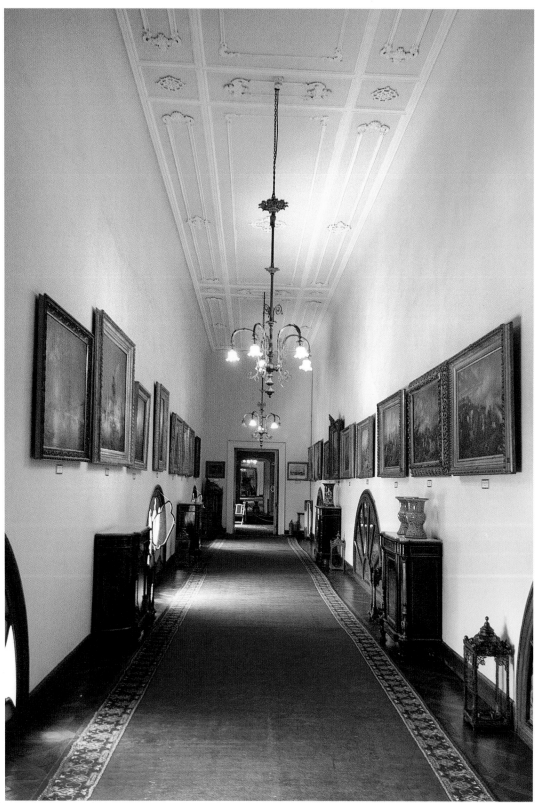

***

Here the Mabeyn building ends and a corridor ornamented with beautiful paintings is followed to pass to the seraglio. The visits in the palace include only some rooms of the Seraglio that are interesting and worth seeing. The kadınefendi chambers as well as master and concubine rooms are outside the visit program because of technical difficulties in their visit. We will finish the palace visit with Muayede Lounge that will be arrived after seraglio and which is no doubt the largest, the most beautiful and glorious lounge of the palace.

***

Seraglio Corridor and paintings

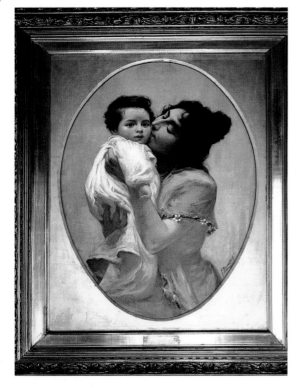

c) Seraglio

Seraglio, in Ottoman palace culture and tradition, is the dominancy area of sultan's mother, that is Sultana. So much so that, the largest place after Hünkar Sofrası was allocated to Sultana. Sultana was responsible from both the guardianship of dynasty family and organizing the daily work at harem. In order to provide this, she had the necessary amount of helpers and an important amount of allowance. In the organization at seraglio, after Sultana, there was Kadın Efendi who was the wife of the sultan with the higher rank. The comments of foreign sources that the power at seraglio was in their wives' hands (haseki) are not really true. This could only happen in cases

73

when the mother of a sultan died before he ascended the throne. Sultanas, having a political authority could be seen only rarely when their child ascended the throne at a very early age. Nevertheless, Ottoman Palace culture and tradition had very strict rules regarding these.

Seraglio of Dolmabahçe Palace connects to Mabeyn building with the corridor that we mentioned above. The women of the seraglio could watch the ceremonies and religious celebrations from the windows of this corridor lying through Muayede lounge. Seraglio section of the palace starts at the end of this corridor.

The window that the seraglio women watched the ceremonies at Muayede Lounge

Women at Seraglio

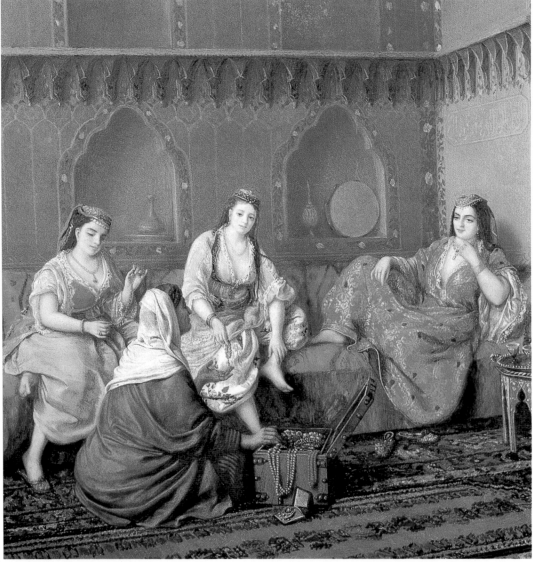

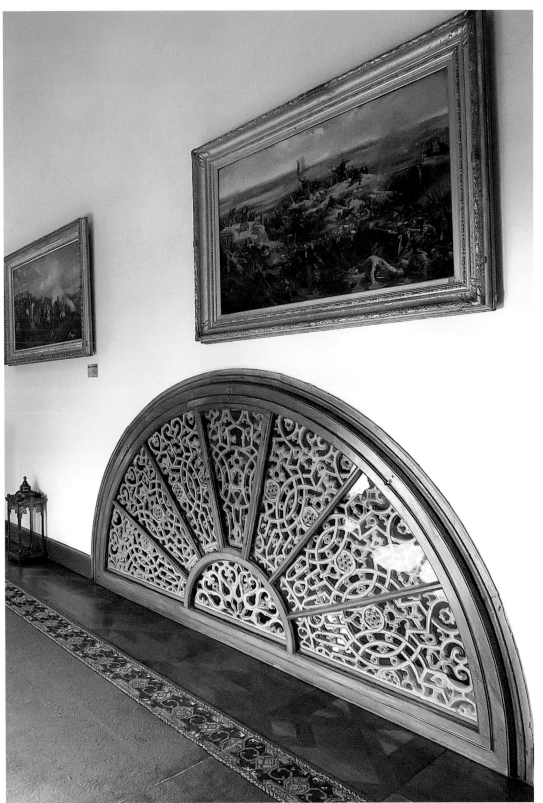

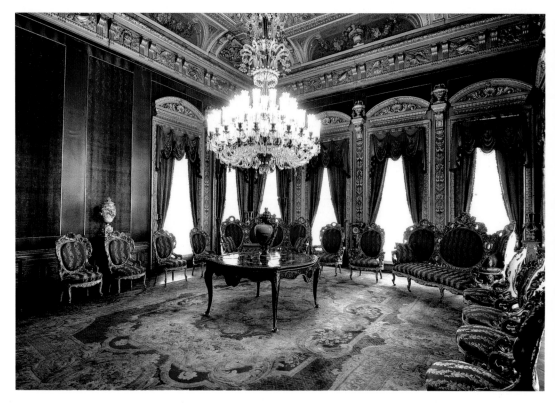

Acceptance Room (Red Room)

Acceptance Room (Red Room)

Right after the doors opening to the seraglio, there is a large room that is carefully decorated and used mostly as a guest hosting location. This room was also named as Red Room because the color red is dominant in the room; it is one of the most beautiful locations of the seraglio. This room – or lounge – was generally used in hosting the lady guests or wives of pasha or ambassadors who came to visit the sultan. The fire place with mirrors ornamented with marble as well as the chandelier of Baccarat crystals of a red line draws attention immediately.

Guest bedroom

Right next to this acceptance room, there is a relatively small room turned into a bedroom for Atatürk's guests who stayed at the palace for the night during the Republican times. Sakal-ı Şerif which is among the relics and believed to belong to Hz. Muhammed, the prophet of Islam, was kept in this small room during the period of Sultan Abdülaziz. The valuable goods in this room are the large bed ornamented with golden gild and the jewelry box displayed at its foot side as well as the beautiful Hereke carpet covering the floor.

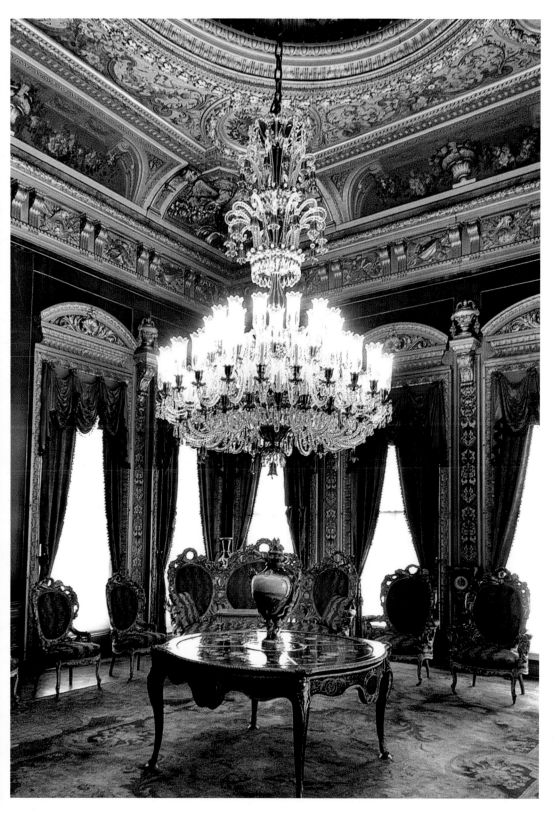

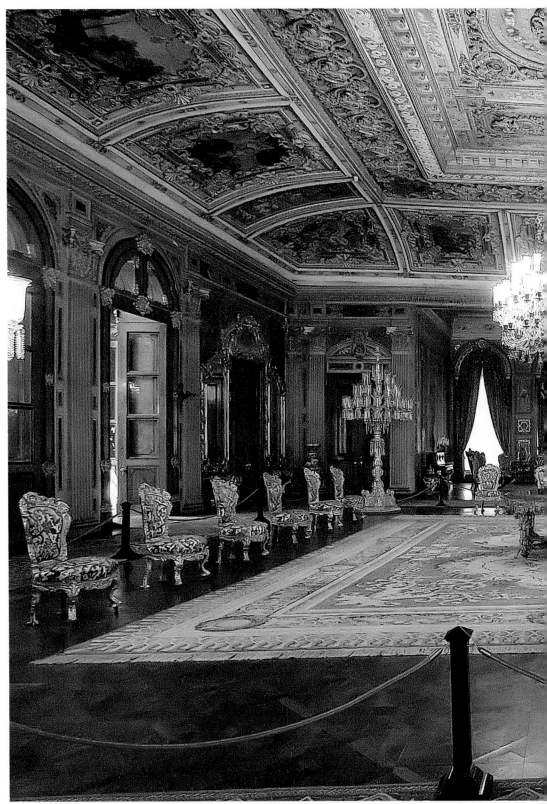

Seraglio Ceremony Lounge (Blue Lounge)

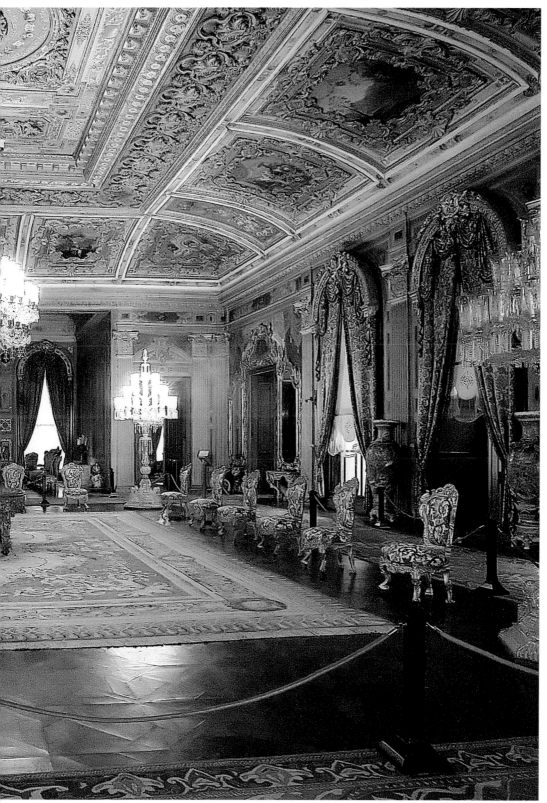

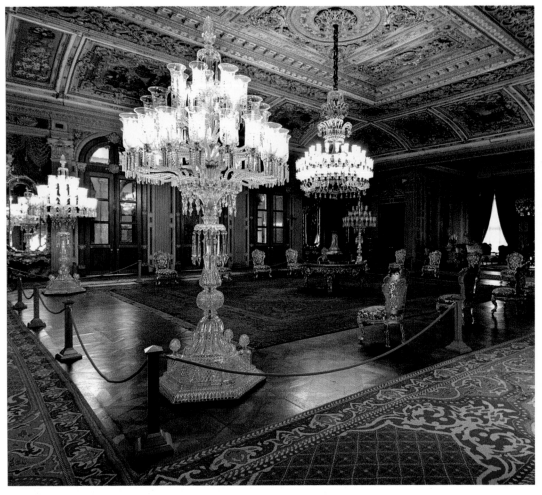

Seraglio Ceremony Lounge (Blue Lounge)

Seraglio Ceremony Lounge (Blue Lounge)

The first large lounge of the seraglio section at this side is the location with a rich decoration, named as Blue Lounge due to the dominant color of the seating groups, curtains and decoration in the two sided lounge of Mabeyn building (Zülveçheyn Lounge). The sultans, after ascending the throne, accepted the congratulations of the ladies from seraglio in this lounge. During the religious ceremonies made in seraglio, this lounge was used. There are many sources and witnesses expressing that these ceremonies with the musicians and ladies chorus were very glorious. The walls ornamented with the natural paintings representing the seasons as well as the ceiling decorated with golden gild increase the glory of the lounge. In the middle of the ceiling, there is a gorgeous chandelier with 72 arms made of Baccarat crystals. Again the four crystal chandeliers used in the illumination of this beautiful lounge have a beauty worth seeing.

The bedroom of Sultana

Right by the lounge, the room on the sea side was used as the bedroom of the mother of the sultan. The bed and wardrobe of gold ornamented elegantly with gild looks magnificent. Again in this room, the magnificent pearl drawer draws attention immediately. The pink atlas curtains and a marble table enriched with gold ornamentation complete the decoration of the room.

Atatürk chamber

In this section of the palace, the two rooms that open to the Ceremony Lounge of the seraglio are the study and the bedroom where Atatürk died. These two rooms were used by the sultan himself as study during the dynasty period. These two rooms that were re-decorated during Atatürk period have a very different plainness and modesty, very different from the decor and organization concept of the time of the sultan. The small and elegant study is among the most notable goods of the study. The Hereke carpet on the floor has a stunning beauty.

Study of Atatürk

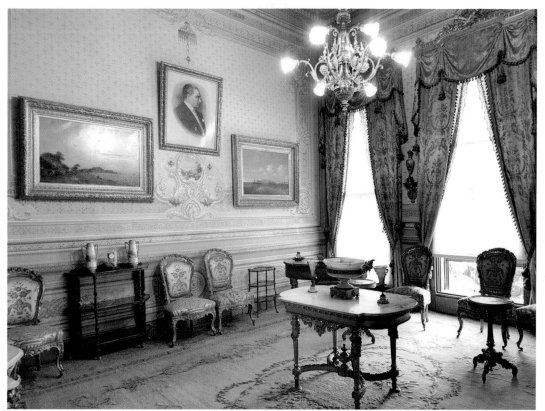

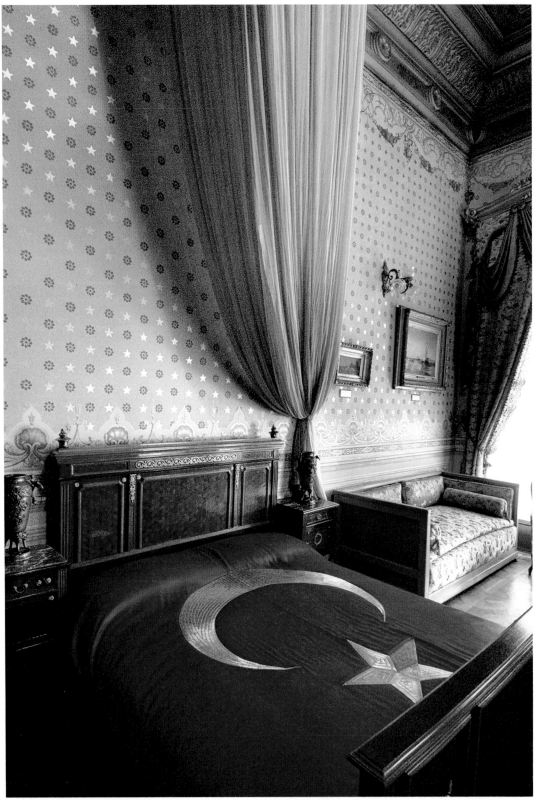

Bed of Atatürk

The other room was used as a bedroom of the sultans for the winter because it could relatively be better heated, before central heating was placed in the palace during dynasty times. It shows a modesty reflecting the humble character of Atatürk. The great leader Atatürk who is the founder of Turkish Republic died at this bed in the morning of 10th, November, 1938 at 9.06. For his memory, all the clocks in the palace were stopped at this time.

Right across this bedroom, there is the bathroom made in the 1910's (during the period of Mehmet Reşat V) and used by Atatürk as well.

The chamber of Abdülaziz and his bedroom

This bedroom which is among the most beautiful bedrooms of the palace is right across the part that Atatürk used over the garden façade of the palace. The decoration of this room, ornamented with a very elegant fireplace with porcelain inlaid and illuminated by a Baccarat chandelier with a skillful craftsmanship, is completed with a gorgeous wardrobe and a multi-functional, comfortable armchair.

The chamber of Abdülaziz and his bedroom

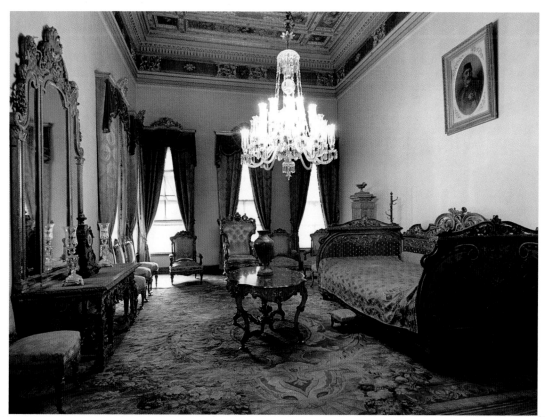

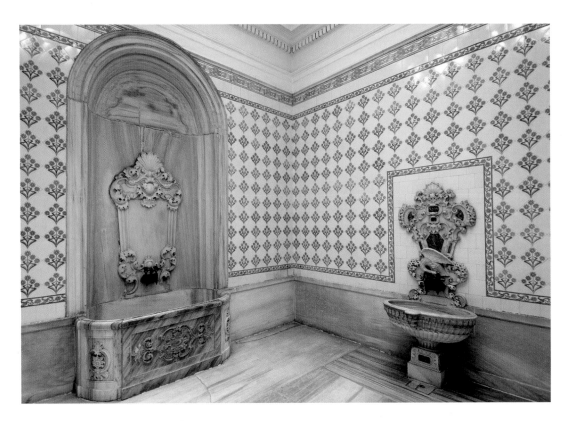

Views of hammams in seraglio section

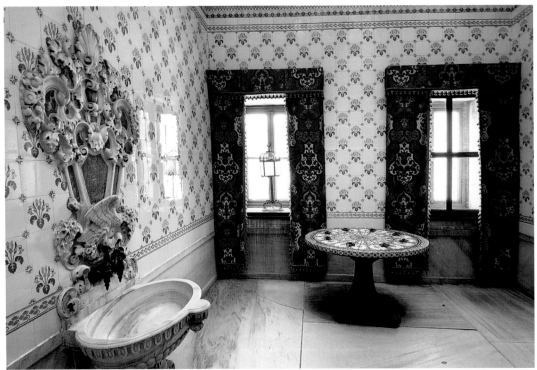

Sultan's hammam

Right by this chamber, there is a sultan hammam which traditionally has three parts (resting room, hot room and cold). The marble basin of the washing place, called as hot room that has marble carving craftsmanship as well as the china stove in the resting section are among the goods of Sultan hammam that are worth seeing.

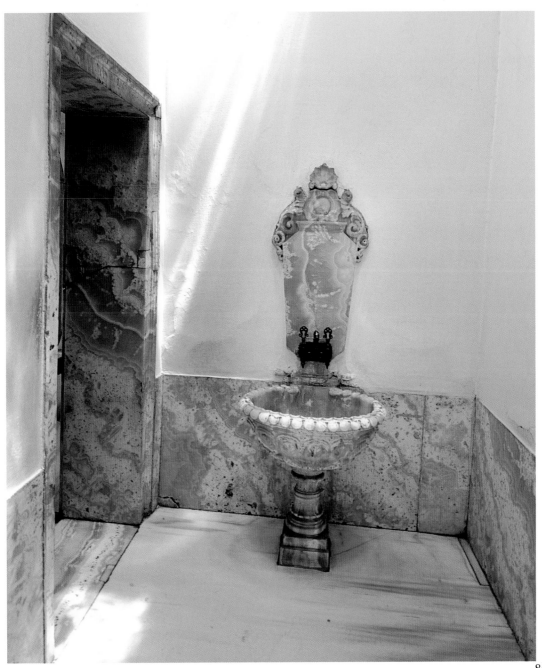

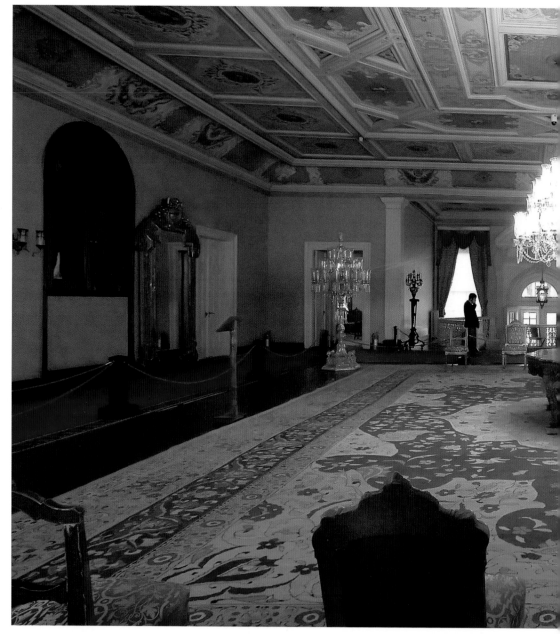

Seraglio Lounge with Two Rooms

Seraglio Lounge with Two Rooms

Here, when returned to the ground floor through caliph stairs, one may descend to the Lounge with Two Doors or Seraglio Passage Lounge as the name used in the palace. It is an important lounge that has passage on the one hand to seraglio garden and seraglio door of the palace on the side of the land; and on the other side towards the sea, to the door of the port. The magnificent chandeliers in this room made of Baccarat crystals and the local made chandeliers on the two sides of the door are perfectly beautiful. The gorgeous Hereke carpet

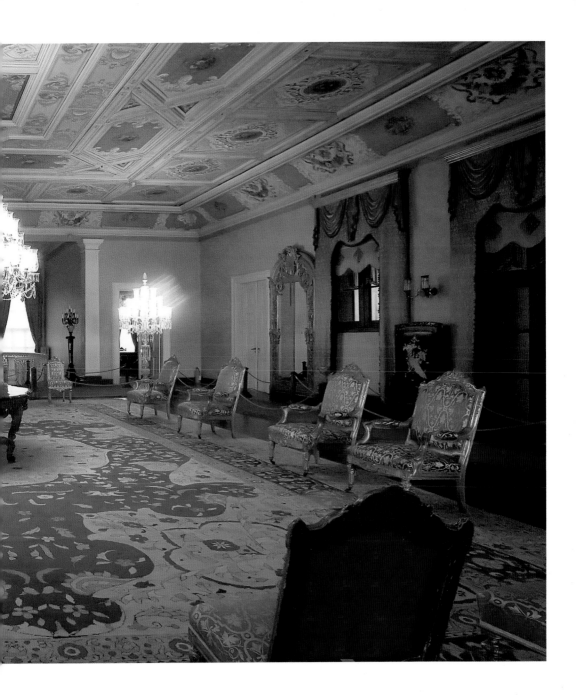

covering the floor of this lounge is among the most beautiful carpets in the palace.

Rooms: Among the rooms that open to this lounge, on the garden side in the left corner, there is a furniture collection which is among the most beautiful examples of Ottoman wooden craftsmanship. The room which is located on the left corner according to the door is called the Room with Pearl due to the materials used abundantly in its decoration. The china stove of Japanese production besides a gorgeous table and cupboards create awe in the viewers.

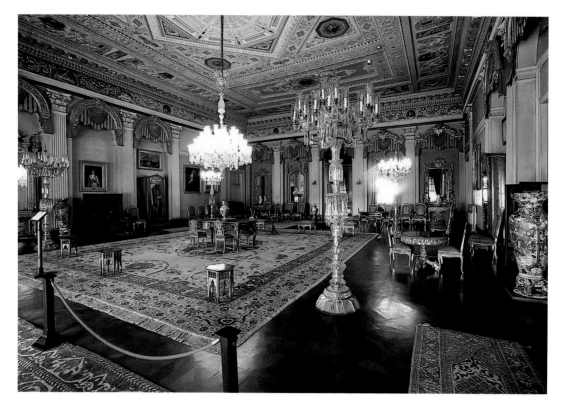

The Hall with Balcony or the Pink Lounge

The Hall with Balcony or the Pink Lounge

This glorious lounge is one of the most beautiful lounges of the seraglio where especially in summer and spring, the Sultana and the wives of the sultans, that is the Kadınefendi, host their relatives who left the palace as a bride. It is learned from the records and some witnesses of the period that sultans have also participated in some of these hosting for visiting their daughters who went as a bride. The balcony of this lounge with a beautiful view was used for sitting and chatting when the weather was suitable. It is known that Atatürk also used this lounge from time to time. The lounge is illuminated with a magnificent chandelier made of Baccarat crystals as well as candlesticks with branches of the same style. The seating group in the style of a corner sofa shall be thought of as a unique example of Turkish-Ottoman seating culture and taste. The silver brazier and the magnificent Hereke carpet that ornament the floor complete the beauty of this lounge.

Sultana's Resting Room

The room in the left corner of the Hall with Balcony used to be a location where the Sultana used for private meetings. It was turned into a complete resting room with the bed group

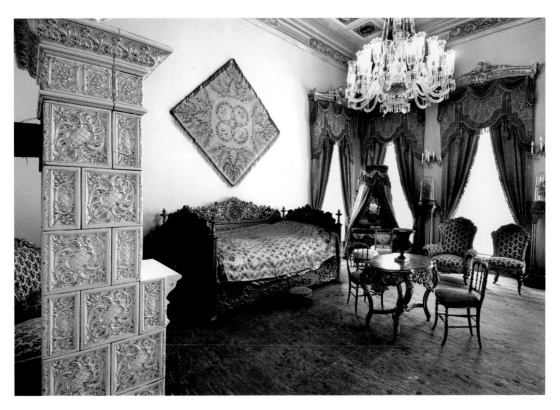

Bedrooms

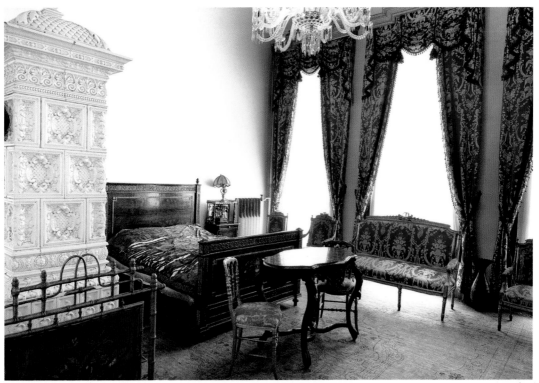

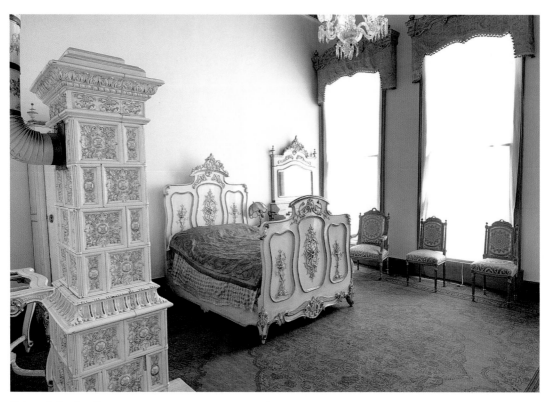

Sultana's Resting Room

Japan Lounge Bedroom of Sultan Mehmet Reşat

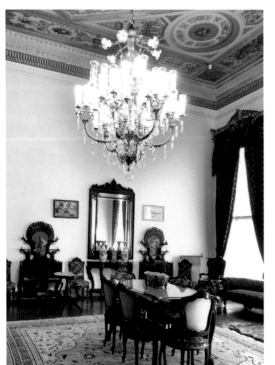

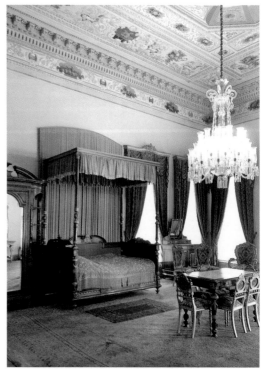

that was placed afterwards. The engravings on the ceiling are among the most beautiful ones of its kind. The room next to this one which is relatively smaller used to be the bedroom of Pertevniyal Sultana who is the mother of Sultan Abdülaziz. It was used as a guest's bedroom after a separate room was organized for Sultana.

Other rooms and lounges

The striking and wide room decorated with furniture from Far-East is named as "Japanese Room" because of its decoration. The first of the two rooms next to it which has a façade towards the sea was also used as the bedroom of Sultana during different periods and carry a light and spacious air with its varnished furniture of creamy white. The larger room next to this constituting the corner on the façade of the sea is the bedroom of Sultan Mehmet Reşat.

***

The sea facade of the seraglio building ends here and the corridors and rooms after this follow each other on the side of the land. All these locations and rooms after this one lounge that provides the connection of the sections before and after this were decorated with a very delicate and elegant taste and is worth seeing. It is as if attention was given to placing a different color to each room: Pink Room, Yellow Room...The golden colored furniture of the yellow furniture, the magnificent Hereke carpet and the glorious crystal chandelier are especially worth stating. There are many beautiful and distinguished paintings on the walls of the lounges and locations. Right after the sofa that provides the passage, the chamber on the right belonged to Leading Kadınefendi. Right across it, there is the hammam of the seraglio. This hammam for the common usage of many seraglio women was organized in two separate hammams with its wide and spacious resting room and the hot sections that constitute the bathing location. The thin Orient carpet of the resting room made of silk and the china stove are among the most beautiful examples of their kind.

The rooms and chambers on the two sides of this upper floor of the seraglio end with a chamber that is elegantly decorated and spacious at the end of the building. At the bottom of this lounge, on the ground floor there is the entrance room of the seraglio. The piece that attracts the greatest attention of the upper lounge is a magnificent Japanese wardrobe and the gorgeous chandelier among the beautiful goods of the ground floor. Again the rooms that open to these lounges have been decorated with extraordinary taste. On the left side, the green china stove at the end of the building is among the most beautiful one of its kind. We would like to pay special attention to many beautiful and valuable carpets in nearly all the rooms of the seraglio.

***

We can stop the seraglio tour here and continue with one of the most magnificent section of Dolmabahçe Palace which is the Great Ceremony Room known better as Muayede Lounge.

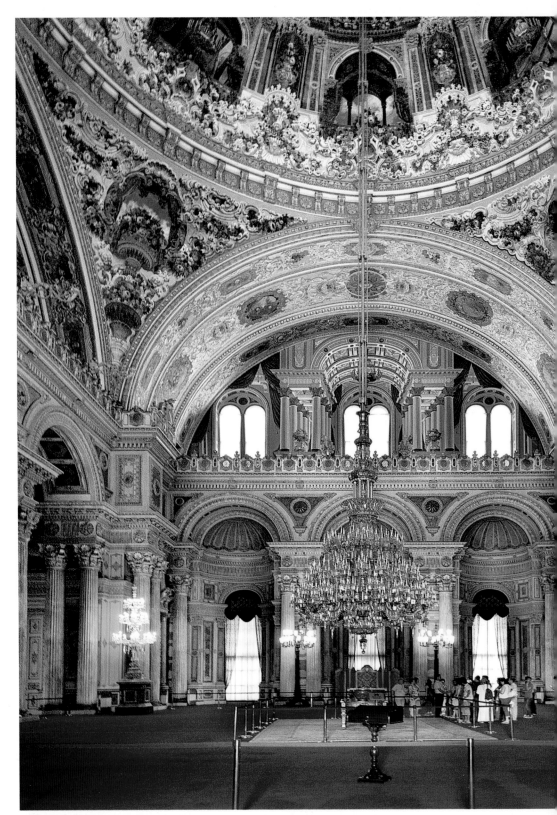

Muayede lounge

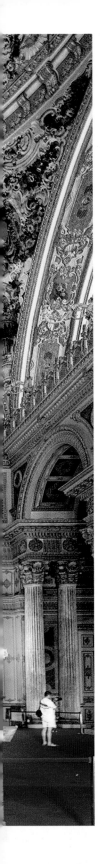

d)Muayede lounge

A grandeur difficult to tell and maybe even impossible without seeing: Here is the masterpiece of architecture and decoration leaving every spectator in awe without an exception! Muayede Lounge that is located between Mabeyn and Seraglio sections of Dolmabahçe Palace and that constitutes the highest part is like a symbol of unique grandeur with its size of 40x45 m2 and with the adjacent places, the area over 2000m2, magnificent crystal chandelier that is nearly 5 tons in weight and with the largest one piece carpet in the world. This marvelous chandelier has 750 crystal illumination elements. Besides, on the sides of the lounge, again there are 4 more chandeliers of crystal. With the dome ceiling cover placed on 56 columns, it seems to symbolize the glory of Ottoman Empire that was already left in the past. The height of this dome is measured as 36 meters. Over the walls, there are pastel colors, and vibrant colors are dominant on the ceiling. In a very well definition about the ceiling ornamentation, it is said that: "The ceiling of Dolmabahçe Muayede Lounge is like a window of the sky and heaven opened to the universe of angels and flowers" (Çelik Gülersoy, Dolmabahçe Palace, p. 208).

This glorious lounge that was first opened in 1856 with the feast that the sultan Abdülmecit held in honor of Marshal Pellissier, the commander of French army in Crimean War, also witnessed the first meeting of national assembly in 1877 due to the announcement of First Constitutional Monarchy. Welcoming and hosting many foreign guests took place at the splendid atmosphere of this lounge.

The balconies on the upper floor are connected to the main location with the carrier elements. This balcony or galleries were allocated to the diplomats, palace orchestra and the invitees. The golden throne exhibited at Topkapı Palace Museum treasury section was brought to this lounge in Bayram and Cülus (ascending the throne) ceremonies and placed on the land side of the lounge towards the sea. A system that blows hot weather from the bottom of the columns enabled the temperature of the location reach to a reasonable point even in the coldest seasons.

The main function of the lounge was the bayram ceremonies as can be understood from its name. According to this, the sultan withdrew to the resting room located at the sea side of Muayede Lounge and stayed here until the people who would participate in the ceremony took their place. Even Abdülhamit II who spent nearly all of his reign of 33 years at this palace did not change this tradition and every year, he participated in the ceremonies in this lounge on the two great religious Bayrams of the year, Ramadan and Kurban. According to this, after everybody took their place in the great lounge, the Sultan entered the lounge upon the invitation of the Head Officer, sat on the golden throne and accepted the congratulations. These ceremonies that took place with the participation of hundreds of distinguished civil and military people took long hours.

After Atatürk, the founder and leader of Turkish Republic died in this lounge on November 10th, 1938, his sacred coffin was placed in a catafalque that is founded in this lounge. He was sent away to eternity from here by countless number of foreign statesmen and hundreds of thousands of people of İstanbul who came there for days.

e)Exhibition rooms

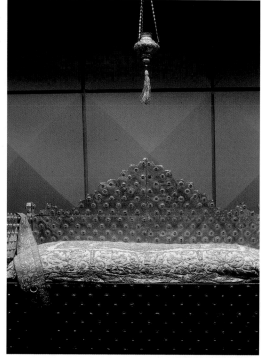

The golden throne displayed at Topkapı Palace

At the Dolmabahçe Palace, there are four exhibition rooms two of which are inside the main palace building and two of which are in auxiliary buildings. On the sea side of the great ceremony room (Muayede room), in the lounges on both sides, valuable goods are exhibited constituting the palace collections. The location used as an Inner Treasury during Ottoman dynasty times is organized as Ottoman Clocks Museum today. The Mansion with Glass that we will state finally is like a separate museum with its goods and decoration as a living location that the sultans used apart from the main palace location.

In the first room on the side of Mabeyn room, there are some personal goods, writing kit, pens, sign and coffee set of Sultan Mehmet Reşat as well as crystal pieces, tea sets, spoons of different materials etc. In the small room next to this room, there are various sultan swords and silver decorations. Opaline and porcelain sets are worth seeing.

At the second exhibition room on the side of harem and again at the sea side, there are elegant crystal and porcelain tea and coffee sets that carry the most famous and distinguished brands abroad as well as various tools, basin and watering can sets, drinking sets, decanter and glasses as well as dynasty signs. Some sets are among the most distinguished products of Yıldız Porcelain factory that is founded in connection with the palace. Besides, on some displays, some personal goods such as combs, cigarette-holders, drinking sets and chess sets can be seen.

The clocks exhibition was organized at the location used as Inner Treasury under the name Ottoman Clocks Museum. This location stands at the point that connects the garden of the seraglio to the palace wall. In the inner treasury building that consists of three rooms side by side, there are many beautiful and important clocks displayed made in Turkey or brought from abroad.

The Mansion with Glass that is organized more like a living room, a resting room rather than an exhibition room is located at the back side of the garden adjacent to the walls of the palace. The entrance room that is ornamented with rich wall ornaments but still decorated in a more plain way is followed by a large main location or sitting room. The furniture, the curtains, carpet and crystal chandelier of this room where royal red is dominant are all distinguished items. Column chandeliers and an ornamented crystal piano complete the decoration of the room. An important part of the illuminated location that gives its name to the mansion with glass is no doubt the glasshouse that is located right in the middle with its pool. The corridor that connects the mansion with glass to the palace is evaluated as an exhibition room. There are still pictures of birds in this corridor.

**

The visit of Dolmabahçe palace ends here. However, as we have stated at the beginning of this book, Clock Tower and Dolmabahçe Mosque, the surrounding of which is used as the parking space constitutes a whole with the Ottoman architecture of 19th century. For this reason, including the monumental doors of the palace, we sincerely advice to elaborate the visit a little further.

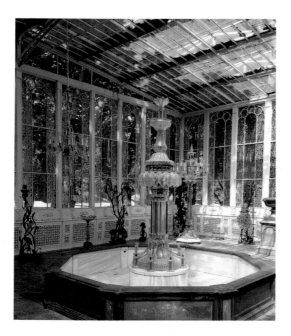
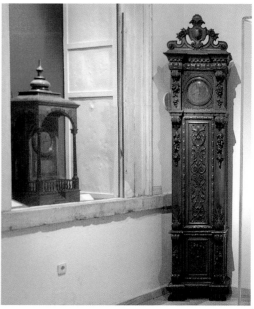

CONTENTS

Published and Distributed by
Duru Basım Yayın Reklamcılık ve Gıda San. Tic. Ltd. Şti.
Ticarethane Sok. Teyfik Kuşoğlu İşhanı No: 41/6
Sultanahmet - İSTANBUL
Tel: (0.212) 527 49 95 Fax: (0.212) 527 95 30
www.durubasim.com.tr info@durubasim.com.tr
Photos : *Erdal Yazıcı, Mahmut Akkaya, Kemal Özdemir Dia Bank*
Typesetting :
Printed in Turkey by : *istanbul ofset*
© *Copyright 2007 **Duru Basım Yayın Reklamcılık ve Gıda San. Tic. Ltd. Şti.***
All rights reserved
ISBN 978-9944-767-08-8